catification

catif

ication

DESIGNING A HAPPY AND STYLISH HOME FOR YOUR CAT (AND YOU!)

Jackson Galaxy

Kate Benjamin

JEREMY P. TARCHER/PENGUIN | A MEMBER OF PENGUIN GROUP (USA) | NEW YORK

JEREMY P. TARCHER/PENGUIN
Published by the Penguin Group
Penguin Group (USA) LLC
375 Hudson Street
New York, New York 10014

USA • Canada • UK • Ireland • Australia
New Zealand • India • South Africa • China

penguin.com
A Penguin Random House Company

Most Tarcher/Penguin books are available at special quantity discounts for bulk purchase for sales
promotions, premiums, fund-raising, and educational needs. Special books or book excerpts also can
be created to fit specific needs. For details, write: Special.Markets@us.penguingroup.com.

Library of Congress Cataloging-in-Publication Data

Galaxy, Jackson.
Catification : designing a happy and stylish home for your cat (and you!) / Jackson Galaxy, Kate
Benjamin.
p.   cm.
ISBN 978-0-399-16601-3 (paperback)
1. Cats—Housing.   2. Cats—Equipment and supplies.   3. Interior decoration.   I. Benjamin, Kate.   II. Title.
SF447.3.G35   2014   2014019022
636.8'083—dc23

Printed in the United States of America
10 9 8 7 6 5 4 3 2 1

Book design by Meighan Cavanaugh

For all the people who have brought cats into their

lives, and to the cats who inspired and challenged

those humans to change the way they live.

contents

a note from jackson

It's a great time to be "the cat guy."

When I started out my life working with animals, around 1993, it was at a shelter in Boulder, Colorado. Within weeks of realizing that the cats had something they wanted to tell me, the other staff members seemed to smell a cat person in their presence. They immediately christened me "Catboy," and put me on the job of decoding everything about cats for everybody. Good thing I was up for the challenge.

Back then, the sense of cats being "other" from humans was clearly prevalent. I mean, if shelter workers were scratching their heads about cat behavior, imagine what the rest of the world was thinking (or not). As a matter of fact, as my knowledge base grew and I refined my techniques, I branched out to other shelters to find the same desperately inquisitive population. You will never find a more compassionate lot than those who dedicate their lives to caring for homeless animals. That said, we were in dire straits. We were labeling as "unadoptable" cats who were acting out from a place that not enough people understood. In the reality of that time, "unadoptable" meant "euthanized." If that didn't give Catboy a sense of urgency, nothing would.

As I left the shelter to pursue private practice, I was constantly up against a seemingly unsolvable puzzle: guardians cared enough to hire me instead of "getting rid of the cat," and that was fantastic; at the same time, however, the suggestion that problems could be remedied by adding more litter boxes, toys, and trees (and, of course, not hiding them in the basement) was a distinctly unwelcome one. We wanted the problem gone, but the solution was aesthetically *painful* to most. Almost all of the guardians I came in contact with were panicked that if I had my way, I would turn their home into the "crazy cat lady house."

Of course, that sense of aesthetic panic on the part of my clients panicked me. It wasn't just a matter of not wanting a litter box in the living room; it symbolized a lack of true empathy toward, and an investment in, *love for* cats. We could easily bear the notion of spreading dog blankets, toys, dishes, beds and stinky rawhides around our house. We wouldn't ask to hide our dogs' existence any more than we would try to hide our children. In the meantime, cats, and the smallest perceptible evidence that they actually lived in our homes, rode squarely in the back of the domestic bus.

In the ensuing twenty years, I've been privileged to witness the cat renaissance; those that were considered "other"—alien, aloof, more furniture than family—are enjoying a surge in popularity like no other time in their "domesticated" history. We hungrily devour cat memes, watch cat videos by the tens of millions (even creating celebrities out of those video cats) and, thankfully for those of us in the rescue community, adopt them in record numbers. The animal that for tens of thousands of years enjoyed a great reputation as a working animal—controlling rodents on farms, for instance—has become a bona fide companion.

A truly amazing bonus to being seen as a companion is that under the surface we are asking not only what we can do for cats to make their lives better, but we are acknowledging what they do for us. Cats are now seen by millions as supportive family members, bearers of unconditional love. We better understand that cats don't show love and devotion like dogs do, and so we invest in the time needed to learn a new language.

You may think of *Catfication* as a design book; it is so much more than that. In the same way that our refusal to add litter boxes symbolized cat shame, what you will see in this book symbolizes cat love. It doesn't illustrate what lengths "those crazy cat people" will go to, but rather the maturation of us as humans. At the very core of my belief system is the knowledge that a meaningful relationship with the animal world completes us as humans. The concept of "dominion," of a natural order of things that has us dominating cats with an iron fist and without regard to their physical, emotional, and spiritual needs, is simply an old way of thinking. I jokingly say that successfully living with cats relies on your ability to compromise. Learning the language of cats, and changing up our environment to accommodate them, to me, is a symbol of our evolution, as it demonstrates our willingness, on a deep level, to compromise for the sake of an animal's happiness.

And where does that leave us? In a pretty good place.

I hope you believe that what you hold in your hands is something far beyond a design book. It's a celebration. A home that proudly advertises that you care about your own comfort as well as that of your animal companions is beautiful to some, but for shelter workers, rescuers, foster parents, and others, it's a moment to shed a tear of gratitude. Cats have cleared a significant hurdle in their timeline. And make no mistake, that timeline has been a rough one. Does *Catfication* mean that we're on our way to becoming like the ancient Egyptians, deifying and burying cats alongside our human family members? Maybe not. Elevating cats, however, means we care not only about the ones in our homes, but *all of them*. We are beginning to care—not just on the lunatic fringe but across the human spectrum—about whether they live or die. And that means more will live. Soon, millions fewer every year will die. And *that* makes it a good time to be the Catboy.

introduction

A friendly greeter at the front door. A fuzzy bed warmer on a cold night. A purring companion curled up on your lap. Living with cats gives us a certain pleasure no other animal companion can provide. Cats are elegant, intelligent, loving creatures that have entered our homes and our hearts. In return for what they give us, we, as responsible cat guardians, must provide them with the things they need to live in a happy, healthy, safe, and stimulating environment.

Keeping cats indoors is the best way to ensure they live long, healthy lives. Yes, cats have natural instincts, such as climbing and hunting, which can be fulfilled when they go outside, but the dangers far outweigh the benefits. Outdoor cats face threats from cars, poisons, being trapped or locked in places they shouldn't be, fights with other outdoor animals, and further unthinkable outcomes. We're here to tell you that you can (and should) keep your beloved feline family members safely indoors, and that you can easily give them all the things they need to thrive. That is what Catification is all about.

The Catification process starts by understanding how your cat sees the world.

Consider yourself the designer and your cat, your client. It's your responsibility to understand your client's needs and preferences. We introduce you to the concept of "cat mojo" in this book, giving you all the tools you need so you can think (and more important, *feel*) like your feline.

In Part 1, we first show you how cats in general are hardwired to see their environment. Then we help you discover your own cat's specific preferences. Armed with this new information, you will be inspired to enhance your cat's environment to accommodate his or her likes and dislikes, encourage positive behaviors, and discourage negative ones.

Part 2 offers a full range of project ideas and inspiration for creating a well-designed and cat-friendly home that provides your cat with the stimulation he or she needs in a way that makes you happy, too. Please don't think you have to cover everything in your house with beige carpet to Catify! That is definitely not the case. You can live with a cat and still have a home you are proud to show off. Catification comes in every style; it just takes a little inspiration and creativity.

Catification doesn't have to be a huge undertaking. It can be as simple as rearranging some furniture. We show you a variety of projects, including many that are easy and inexpensive. We hope you will find something to inspire you at the level where you are comfortable—whatever your skill or budget.

Why Catify?

Catification has immediate and obvious benefits for both you and your cat. Many behavior problems can be reduced or even eliminated with the introduction of certain environmental enhancements. Catification is essential, whether you have one cat or several, but in a multi-cat household, it is especially critical. It's the only way to keep the peace among multiple cats living in the same home. Environmental enhancements give everyone the space they need to coexist and live peacefully, even in a very small living space. Catified homes can reduce stress levels for all occupants—human, feline, canine, etc. Lowering stress can reduce health problems and even increase life expectancy, for everybody.

Ultimately, if your cat is happier, you will be happier, too, and the bond between you will deepen.

It is our hope that the information and ideas in this book will inspire more people to bring cat companions into their homes and their lives. We are facing an enormous pet overpopulation problem in the United States, and cats more frequently suffer the consequences than any other animal. We feel Catification is one of the key factors in changing this trend. If cat guardians can understand how their cats see the world and make the necessary changes to accommodate those preferences, more cats will stay in happy forever homes, and fewer will be sent to shelters or, worse, outside to fend for themselves.

Opening your heart and your home to a cat companion (or two!) is one of the most rewarding things you can do.

Let's Catify!

Jackson and Kate

understanding catification

the raw cat

Cats are hardwired to see the world a certain way. If you take the time to understand your cat's perspective, it will be much easier to Catify your home. Of course, every cat is different, and we get to that in an upcoming chapter, but first, let's put on our cat glasses and take a look at how and why cats see their environment the way they do.

Who Is the Raw Cat?

If you strip away all the trappings of the modern domestic housecat—the fancy beds, the cushy lifestyle, the food on demand—what's left is the Raw Cat, essentially a wild animal who is a dedicated, carnivorous hunter, and an animal positioned firmly in the middle of the food chain; in other words, every one of his or her senses is honed as both predator and prey. The Raw Cat always has one eye open—whether hunting, securing resources, defending his or her territory, or even sleeping and eliminating. It's all done with the sharpened senses of kill or be killed. Watch your cat come to life as he spots a moth on the ceiling or a bird outside the window—that's the Raw Cat engaging prey. Observe your cat's eyes, ears, and musculature as she sees another cat enter the room—that's the Raw Cat preparing and executing a friend-or-foe kind of threat assessment of her territory. These are the behaviors responsible for the successful propagation of the species for tens of thousands of years.

As you learn more about the Raw Cat and how domestic cats are hard-wired, start observing your cat and ask yourself the following questions:

"How does my cat tap into his or her inner Raw Cat?"

"What does my cat do to demonstrate Raw Cat behavior?"

"Where does my cat demonstrate Raw Cat behavior?"

The Human-Feline Relationship

Cats consistently have been part of human civilization, predominantly as pest control and mainly outdoors. Cats began to interact with humans nearly ten thousand years ago, just as agriculture began to flourish in the Middle East's Fertile Crescent region. The relationship between cats and humans was mutually beneficial. The cats were attracted to the rodents eating the humans' grain, and the humans liked how the cats controlled the rodent population.

The cats' benefit to humans required no selective breeding but was just part of the cats' true nature. Other species of domesticated animals, such as the dog, have been modified through artificial selection to produce specialized breeds for herding, guarding, and hunting. As a matter of fact, it's fair to say cats remain comparatively undomesticated altogether.

Cats lived at the periphery of human society; they cohabitated with people but still retained their independence. Cats only interacted with humans at times of their own choosing, thus retaining strong ties to their wild ways.

It was during the Victorian era that cats began to be thought of as pets and not just as pest control. Queen Victoria was a devoted animal lover and advocate for animal rights. She owned several animals, including two blue Persian cats she adored. Her fascination with cats influenced the public to start bringing cats into their own homes as well.

Even though cats have been brought indoors, their relationship with humans, as well as their nutritional, physical, and emotional needs, remain the same. This journey we've undergone together has left cats relatively unchanged. And the part of this situation that gets under most humans' skin is that cats' primary objective as the Raw Cat has little to do with pleasing us. Ouch.

The Move Indoors

Even though Queen Victoria popularized cats as pets, it was only relatively recently that housecats started transitioning from indoor-outdoor to indoor-only, so the Raw Cat is still adapting to an indoor-only environment. In fact, cats have surpassed dogs as the most common pet in American households. According to the Humane Society of the United States, there are 83.3 million dogs in U.S. homes versus 95.6 million cats. The expanding human population living in urban environments is thought to be one of the reasons for the increase in cats' popularity. Cats are better equipped to live in small spaces, function independently with less help from their caregivers, and co-exist with humans in a busy society.

Cats living indoors are under the charge of their human caretakers. This means guardians control what, when, and where their cats eat, as well as where they use the litter box. Guardians also are responsible for their cats' opportunities to engage in species-appropriate activities. It almost goes without saying that this part of their domestic journey has been the bitterest pill for the Raw Cat to swallow.

Cats are the only true carnivore humans have tried to domesticate, and have gone from having a free-roaming, active existence to a captive, indoor, sedentary one. Cats have gone from frequent consumption of small meals comprised of animals they would catch and kill to a prepared diet of the guardian's choosing. Oftentimes, these meals are offered in excessive amounts and consist of less protein and a wider variety of protein, fat, and carbohydrates than is found in wild birds, insects, and small rodents. Most often, cats are not fed meals at all but instead are "free fed"—left to graze all day even though their bodies are designed for exactly the opposite.

Cat guardians who try to get their cats to adapt to their human lifestyle and preferences without considering cats' true nature and needs will likely find themselves with an unhappy cat who exhibits what the guardian deems undesired behavior problems. A cat guardian must try to understand how domestication affects his or her cat's behavior, well-being, and health.

Research shows that many of the chronic health problems domestic cats face are directly or indirectly related to not only nutrition but also lifestyle changes that have been imposed on cats by their guardians.

The news is not all bad for cats. The average life span has increased from 4.5 years for cats who live outdoors to nearly fifteen years for indoor cats who also have preventative medical care. That said, we believe we needn't make any compromises at all; we can have our vision of what cats should be in our homes while simultaneously allowing the Raw Cat to flex his or her mind/body muscles.

Catification accommodates the Raw Cat, and it does so in a way everyone can live with. When the cat guardian takes the time and effort to create a healthy, stimulating environment for their wild carnivore living indoors, both cat and guardian will enjoy a happy life together.

Cat Senses

Because cats experience the world as both predator and prey, cat behavior and communication is geared toward preventing altercations over food and territory, as well as other skirmishes. It is important to remember cats' perception of the world is based on their senses, most of which are more acute than our own.

VISION

Cats' visual field of view is about 200 degrees, compared to 180 degrees in humans. As a predator, cats' eyes face forward, allowing for depth perception. While humans have more acute central vision, cats' eyes are adapted to detect movement quickly, even in the dimmest of light. This ability is part of what makes cats successful hunters. It is important to remember that rapid movement, especially if it is unexpected, will heighten a cat's response. As a matter of fact, a new study from biologists at City University in London shows that cats and dogs can see ultraviolet light.

TOUCH

Cats have highly sensitive slow- and fast-acting hair follicle receptors. These are responsible, in some cats, for an aggressive response to even the gentlest petting. This response is also known as petting-induced overstimulation aggression.

Cats have about twenty-four movable whiskers in four sets on each upper lip on both sides of the nose. They also have whiskers on each cheek; over their eyes; and on their chin, inner wrist, and back of their legs. The information sent back to their brain from their whiskers enables cats to create a three-dimensional map of their surroundings without actually seeing it.

HEARING

Cats hear a broader range of frequencies, including ultrasound. Cats can hear sounds humans cannot hear on both ends of the spectrum and especially the higher end. Cats' ears are designed to draw sound into the ear canal, and their movable pinnae help locate the sound. And speaking of movable, cats' ears can rotate an astonishing

300 degrees, functioning as the "eyes in the back of their head" when dealing with life as a preyed-upon animal. Because of the cats' unique ear design, their hearing is more sensitive to the higher amplitude of sound.

SMELL

Cats have an excellent sense of smell, with five to ten times more olfactory epithelium than humans have. Cats also have vomeronasal organs, also known as Jacobson's organs, located in the roof of the mouth behind their upper incisors. The flehmen response, when cats lift their lips and open their mouth to sniff, is often misinterpreted as a sign of aggression, but in fact, it is a normal cat behavior. Cats sniff pheromones in the air and bring them into their mouth, where they are picked up by the Jacobson's organ that sends the information to the hypothalamus in the brain, enabling the cats to analyze other cats or critters in their vicinity.

Cats can easily experience sensory overload. When multiple stressors are present, including sounds, sights, smells, and touches, the accumulation of stress from multiple stimuli can be greater than the sum of the stress from the individual elements.

Cat Body Language

Cats communicate a lot about their mood through their body language. Ears, tail, whiskers, and body posture all give us clues about whether Kitty is pleased or discontent, which indicates confidence or a lack of it. You have to be able to identify when and where your cat is confident or unconfident in order to properly Catify. Of course, not all cats exhibit exactly the same body language; keep in mind that every cat is different. Here are some general examples:

TAIL POSITIONS

Tail Up
A tail straight up or in a question mark indicates that your cat is happy and feeling friendly and welcoming.

Tail Down
A tail down might be a sign your cat is scared or feels threatened, or Kitty could be stalking her prey.

Tail Twitching
If your cat's tail is moving back and forth, she could be trying to assess the situation, or it could indicate that she is agitated.

Tail Bristled

This is a big warning sign that your cat is angry about something. She's making herself look larger and scarier in order to ward off the perceived threat.

EAR POSITIONS

Ears Forward

When your cat is holding her ears forward, it means she is feeling confident, friendly, and playful.

Ears Up

Ears straight up means your cat is alert and paying attention to something in her environment.

Ears Back

Ears back could indicate that your cat is feeling nervous, anxious, or even irritated.

Ears down Flat

Ears flat against the head signal an angry or aggressive cat who is feeling scared and defensive.

WHISKER POSITIONS

Whiskers out to the Side

If your cat's whiskers are out to the side in their natural position, it means she is relaxed and content. Nothing is distracting or upsetting her.

Whiskers Flattened

When your cat's whiskers are held back and flat against her face, she is likely feeling afraid or defensive.

Whiskers Forward

Whiskers pointing forward mean your cat is investigating something. It may also be an indication that she is about to bite whatever is in front of her.

A cat's overall body posture is an excellent indicator of her mood and whether or not she's comfortable in her environment. There's a big difference between a cat who's sprawled out lazily on the living room floor, grooming or napping, and a cat who's cowering under the bed or behind a bookshelf. Let's look at some examples of confident, comfortable cats versus unconfident, scared cats.

Dorling Kindersley/Getty Images

Friendly and Inquisitive

Here comes Kitty, tail in the air, head held high, and ears forward, ready to greet you!

Grigory Bibikov/E+/Getty Images

Relaxed

This is what confidence looks like—a relaxed cat who feels safe and secure.

Jane Burton/Dorling Kindersley/Getty Images

On Alert

If Kitty is walking with her tail down and her ears to the side or back, she's probably being cautious or nervous about something in her environment.

Agitated

Pushed beyond a state of alert, an agitated cat will have his ears back and a body posture that says "Whoa! I'm unhappy here!"

Defensive

Now we've reached fight or flight. Cats who are feeling threatened will puff up to appear larger and display a coiled body posture, ready to spring into action.

cat mojo

mo·jo noun \\'mō-(,)jō\\ :
   a power that may seem magical and that allows someone to be
   very effective, successful, etc.

What Is Cat Mojo?

What is it that motivates cats? What makes them tick? The answer is confident ownership of territory and the instinctive feeling of having a job to do in that territory. This is cat mojo. When a cat really has his mojo on, he will carry out his daily activities of hunting, catching, killing, and eating his prey, followed by grooming and sleeping, all with confidence.

Cat mojo is something all domestic housecats, whom we call family members, inherited from their wildcat ancestors—it's the Raw Cat in all of them. Cat mojo is part of who cats are and has a significant impact on how they experience the world. In the Raw Cat's universe, mojo in action is the key to survival. A confident cat is proactive, while an unconfident cat is reactive. Confident cats have objectives and tasks to complete, while unconfident cats are simply reacting to things happening around them. In short, a mojo-tastic cat is a portrait of confidence in motion.

Each specific cat then has a unique story and set of experiences that affect his or her personal view of the world, but we have to start by understanding cats in general to figure out how we understand our own individual cats.

HUNT, CATCH, KILL, EAT, GROOM, SLEEP

These are the six basic activities that make up cats' natural routines. If a cat is feeling confident in his environment, he will carry out all six activities as part of his daily routine. For indoor cats, we must provide them with an environment and activities that allow them to do these things. This includes offering lots of toys and play to simulate hunting and catching prey, feeding them a species-appropriate, meat-based diet to satisfy their killing and eating instincts, and providing them with comfortable surroundings where they feel at ease enough to groom and sleep.

STUDIO BOX/Photographer's Choice RF/Getty Images

HUNT

CATCH

Allison Achauer/Flickr/Getty Images

©Susan Weingartner Photography

KILL

EAT

Michael J. Hipple/age Footstock/Getty Images

Lisa Stirling/Digital Vision/Getty Images

GROOM

SLEEP

Dernveck Marktisym/Flickr/Getty Images

FIGHT OR FLIGHT: CAT AS BOTH PREDATOR AND PREY

In nature, cats are nowhere near the top of the food chain. As a result, they are always in the mode of simultaneously hunting and being hunted, which in turn has a big impact on how they move through and experience their environment. Cats acting as predators search for potential prey while cats acting as potential prey look out for possible threats and make note of escape routes. Your little lion is trying to avoid being attacked while at the same time seeking out the perfect spot from which to nab her prey.

Today we know cats as social creatures, but they remain solitary hunters at heart. The lone hunter must maintain his or her physical health, and for this reason, cats are made to avoid confrontation. Cats' flight-or-fight instinct is skewed toward flight, so cats will fight only as a last resort. Cats know that to survive as a predator and to avoid becoming prey, they must escape injury.

When cats are panicked, they often go to places where they feel the most protected from their predators. The confident cat knows that panic does not foster wise decisions, and so he avoids it by surveying the room, making note of the comings and goings and possible escape routes, while an unconfident cat will just focus on the escape or the hiding place.

CAT CHESS: SEEING THE WORLD STRATEGICALLY

The kind of militaristic way in which cats see their environment requires a strategic approach, which the environment must accommodate. Cats will look for vantage points from which to survey their surroundings. They will also pay special attention to corners or dead ends.

Blue Balentines/Imagebroker/Getty Images

🐾 Jackson

In a game that involves militaristic strategy, you always have to think three steps ahead. You always have to think about your opponent's next move and how you're going to respond. You're playing out scenarios. You're looking for checkmate (predation) while trying to avoid checkmate (being preyed upon). Now take the concept of what is a "game," and put life or death stakes on it. Now you're thinking like a cat.

OWNERSHIP OF TERRITORY: MAKING A PLAY FOR RESOURCES

One strategic cat move is to claim resources in an environment by marking territorially significant spots. If resources are scarce, cats need to let everyone else know when they have staked their claim. Cats will mark a safe dwelling that provides shelter and access to food and water. They do this with scent and visual marking, like scratching.

Cat Archetypes, Mojo Style

As we've discussed, cat mojo is all about ownership. Life on the territorial spectrum encompasses the vast terrain between displays of confident ownership and unconfident posturing and acting out. With the help of Catification, we strive to help all cats be confident and comfortable in owning their environments. To give you some guidelines, consider these three types of cats:

THE MOJITO CAT (A.K.A. THE HOSTESS WITH THE MOSTEST)

First we have the confident owner of territory, the Mojito Cat. This is the cat that walks into a room, chest held high, tail in the air, with a relaxed posture. She comes right up to you, gives you a little head butt, weaves in and out of your legs, and gives you sweet eyes—she's a picture of territorial confidence. If that cat was human, and you arrived at her house for a cocktail party, she would greet you at the door with a tray of drinks, saying "Welcome to my house! Help yourself to a mojito. Twist of lime? Come on in and I'll give you a tour!" The Mojito Cat represents the essence of cat mojo because she is owning her territory actively, confidently, and in a relaxed way. Her confidence comes from her knowing that everything she has is safely hers.

THE NAPOLEON CAT (A.K.A. THE OVEROWNER)

Next we have the Napoleon Cat. When you encounter this guy, his ears are forward; he's glaring at you with eyes zeroed in just a little; and he's crouching down in an offensive, sometimes even aggressive posture. His initial thought is, *Who are you, and what are you here to steal?* Perhaps he's even lying down across the doorway of the house to ensure you've got to step over that line. Sometimes the Napoleon Cat pees on things because he doesn't trust his ownership of the territory—he needs to mark it.

All beings, whether they're people or animals, who don't confidently own their territory, overown it instead. Think of gangs who "tag" walls with graffiti—they *need* to tell competing gangs (and the world at large) that this wall, this block, this neighborhood belongs to them . . . and don't forget it. The Napoleon Cat is anti-mojo, anti-confidence, because overowning by definition is reactive, not active.

THE WALLFLOWER CAT (A.K.A. THE DISAPPEARING ACT)

While the overowner is lying across the doorway and the mojito cat is walking around shouting, "Hey! How you doing?," there remains the cat hanging back against the wall, never walking across the middle of the floor. The Wallflower Cat is saying, "I don't own this. You must be the owner. Okay, fine, I'm not looking at you, I'm just going to the litter box over there. I'm just leaving. Don't mind me. Good-bye." And, just like that, the Wallflower disappears. Like the Napoleon Cat at the other end of the confidence pendulum, the Wallflower Cat is also anti-mojo because hiding is reactive, not active. It doesn't matter whether or not the threat is real or imagined—it still deserves her full attention and prompt action.

We want all cats to be their version of mojito cats; in other words, not conforming to what we think confidence should look like but acknowledging their tendencies and easing their anxieties to make them the best Mojito Cat they can be. If your cat is a Wallflower, you've got to bring him out a little bit. If he's an overowner, you've got to pull him back a little bit. Why? Because we want all cats to own their territory with confidence—and we believe it's a completely attainable goal.

Figure out who your cat is, watch him walk around the room, watch how he interacts with other cats, humans, the space itself—and figure out who he is. Which cat does he resemble? Does he display confident ownership of his territory, or is he overowning or disappearing?

The Confident Where

Catification is all about creating an environment where your cat is confident and comfortable. Cats assess territory in its entirety; that is to say, they see the entire world, both horizontal and vertical, as space worthy of ownership. Even if your cat is a Napoleon Cat or a Wallflower Cat, you can be sure he finds confidence someplace.

When your cat walks into a room, where is he most confident? Remember, it's all about cat mojo, that inner sense of having a job to do, and, of equal importance, knowing where he does that job best. So if your cat is expressing confidence in his environment, he will be actively surveying the "confident where" of the territory. Somewhere from floor to ceiling you will find him stalking his prey, grooming, or resting. Remember, hiding or becoming small does not signify confidence. The key to confidence is spotting proactivity as opposed to reactivity.

We've broken the confident where into three basic places. When a cat expresses his mojo in one of these places, we call it dwelling. Dwelling equals owning with confidence, and that's exactly what you want to see your cat doing. Let's take a look at the three types of dwellers.

THE BUSH DWELLER

A Bush Dweller is a cat who is confident in spots that are down low and somewhat hidden from view, like under a table or behind a potted plant. From this spot, he can survey his territory, stalk his prey, or simply rest with ease. Think about cats in the wild, hanging out in the bush. They're waiting to hunt, to strike, to pounce. They're down there getting their mojo on. One thing they are *not* doing is hiding; even while hidden, even while perfectly still, the mojorific cat is still *engaged*.

© 2014 Discovery Communications, LLC

Nazra Zahri/Flickr/Getty Images

THE TREE DWELLER

The Tree Dweller isn't on the ground; he's up somewhere in the vertical world. Think about leopards taking their kill up into a tree. Why? Not to hide from everybody but to demonstrate confidence. He's saying, "I feel safe up here. My kill is safe from the other cats down on the ground. And I want the cats on the ground to see what I've done."

Here's the important thing about tree dwelling: it can be anywhere above the ground. Tree dwelling doesn't necessarily mean way up in the rafters. Rafters are

Gallo Images—Daryl Balfour/Riser/Getty Images

included, for sure, but it can also include a chair, a table, or the top of the couch. The key is demonstrating confidence anywhere in the vertical world.

THE BEACH DWELLER

Like the Bush Dweller, the Beach Dweller is also down on the floor, with all four paws planted firmly on the ground; however, Beach Dwellers like being out. This is the cat you trip over every day when you walk into the living room. Just like the leopard eating its prey in the tree, this cat is making a territorial play. Beach dwellers are sending a clear message to you and the other animals in the house that the center of the floor is their territory. They're saying, "If you want to walk through this room, you're going to have to go around me."

The Unconfident Where

THE ANTI-DWELLER

If your cat is under the bed, making himself small and invisible, or cowering on top of the refrigerator, this is not expressing confidence. This is not dwelling. Rather, this is exhibiting fear; it is anti-dwelling. Unconfident cats are in a place of hiding because there's nowhere else for them to be. They're trying to disappear or get away. Here are some anti-dwelling behaviors to look out for:

Caving

Caving is a term for cats that are hiding away out of fear. They are trying to do nothing but vanish. When a cat is caving, he is trying to disappear into a dark, enclosed space where no one can find him. We can allow cats to be tucked away in secluded areas, but we need to control where these places are.

Fridging

This a cat who hides on top of the fridge, or in another place that's up high, to get away from other cats or people in the house who are tormenting him (it doesn't matter whether the torment is real or perceived). He's not coming down because he feels safe only up where he can disappear. It becomes our very important job as guardians to show him that safety does not equal confidence.

© 2014 Discovery Communications, LLC

Of course you want to help your cat transition from caving to bush dwelling, and from fridging to tree dwelling. How do you do that? First and foremost, you Catify. You allow the territory to become his ally. You add features that allow your cat to move around with confidence first in his "comfort zones," and then, over time, encourage him to come out and join the rest of the world. If your cat is displaying the unconfident—fear and the urge to disappear and be small—it's your job to gently push his challenge line, demonstrating to him that he can, with relative ease, move from that place of fear into a confident world that is set up for him to step into his greatness.

The Unders

This is any place that is hidden away, down low—like far under the bed, beneath a chair, or deep in the back of the closet. The unders are places where cats will be found caving. You don't want to see your cat inhabiting these places in fear. Instead you want to draw them out and make them bush dwellers who can still be down low, but in a place of confidence.

Cocooning

When is a cave *not* a cave?
When it's a cocoon! A cocoon is
an enclosed place you control.
It's not under the bed or in
some other unreachable
location. It's a movable cave
you can place in socially
significant areas. True to their
names, cocoons present us with the
magic of metamorphosis, helping
your cat "gain his wings," and
transition from caver to dweller.

Marser/Flickr/Getty Images

getting to know your cat

Now that we've outlined the basic essence of all cats, it's time to get personal and take a closer look at *your* cat. You'll need to identify your cat's specific preferences and personality in order to have the information you need to properly Catify your home.

Know Your Client

Think of yourself as the designer and your cat as your client. The first thing you'll need to do is get a good understanding of who your client is and what his or her environmental preferences are. It's like detective work; you'll have to pay careful attention to what your cat does and how she behaves in different situations and then piece together your findings to get a good understanding of your cat's likes and dislikes.

Every cat has a unique story, and you'll have to figure out the story for your cat. Where did your cat come from? What are her past experiences? Those experiences shape her moment-to-moment present life—how she owns her territory, where she is most confident, and where she is least confident. Remember, this reality can and will change from day to day and over time, but her story, her history informs all of it. That story is the foundation of your Catification plan.

Don't be intimidated by this task—so many of us have adopted cats and have no concrete idea about their actual story, but this is an excuse to write their story with the same confidence as when you gave them their name. All you need to use is your existing bond and a healthy dose of imagination. Get excited! This is the fun part of being a cat guardian; you should be intrigued by these incredible creatures and find their every move fascinating. Just remember that careful observation is the key to creating a truly successful environment for your cat.

KNOW YOUR CAT WORKSHEET

Answer these questions for each cat in your household. You'll need to take the time to observe your cat and really take note of his or her preferences and behaviors. Snap some photos or take a video of your cat in different situations to help you do the analysis. Be a detective, and think like a cat!

Background Info

CAT'S NAME: _____

AGE: _____

Where in your home is your cat confident?

When your cat is down low, is he or she expressing confidence or hiding out? What body language do you observe that helps you draw that conclusion?

_____

_____

Describe the areas where your cat hangs out on the ground. Are they tucked away or out in the open?

_____

_____

When your cat is up high, is he or she expressing confidence or hiding out?

_____

_____

Are there different times of day when your cat prefers different places? Name the places.

_____

_____

When your cat walks into the room, where is he or she looking to go? Are there places she wants to be that she can't get to? How does she behave when she comes into the room? Does she make a beeline to get under the table to hide, or does she immediately jump up on a chair to say hello?

_____

_____

Which type of Dweller do you think your cat is?

Based on your observations, where does your cat demonstrate confidence? It might be in more than one place, so think about all three types of dwellers.

	Not at All	Somewhat	Definitely
Bush Dweller	☐	☐	☐
Tree Dweller	☐	☐	☐
Beach Dweller	☐	☐	☐

Anti-Dwelling behavior

Does your cat ever exhibit either of the anti-Dwelling behaviors?

	Never	Sometimes	Frequently
Caving	☐	☐	☐
Fridging	☐	☐	☐

Who is your cat?

Think about the type of cat yours is, keeping in mind that it might change over time or in different situations. Your cat could be a Napoleon Cat in the morning and a Wallflower at night. Or maybe he's a Mojito Cat when you come home but a Wallflower when visitors come over.

How often does your cat behave like one of the three types of cats?

	Never	Sometimes	Frequently
Mojito Cat	☐	☐	☐
Napoleon Cat	☐	☐	☐
Wallflower Cat	☐	☐	☐

Write your cat's story

Write out the story of your cat, using the first person (tell it in your cat's voice). How do you see the world? What things do you love, and what things do you find threatening? What do you love to do and why? Figure out what makes your cat tick, and bring the story to life.

_____

_____

_____

_____

_____

_____

_____

Every parent has dreams for their children; what are your hopes for your cat? What behaviors do you see now that signify fear and lack of confidence? What would your cat's version of Mojito Cat look like? What would "stepping into her greatness" look like?

_____

_____

_____

_____

_____

_____

_____

_____

get ready to catify!

Now that you understand cats in general and your cat specifically, it's time to translate the information you've gathered into an environmental plan that caters to your cat's needs. Here are some of the key concepts of Catification, which we demonstrate with examples in Part 2.

Urban Planning

Think of Catification like urban planning. It's a process for designing an urban environment (your home) to accommodate the needs of the residents (you, your family, your cat, and any other animals residing there), so everyone can coexist in an orderly fashion. One of the biggest concerns of urban planning is traffic flow, and that's the same for Catification. Everyone must be able to move freely through the space without conflict.

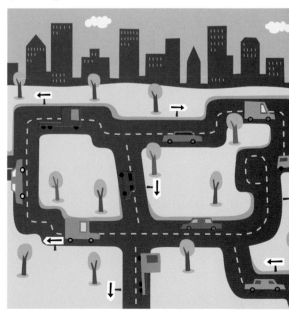

Amathers/iStock Vectors/Getty Images

. . .

When looking at the traffic flow in your home, consider resolving the following "red flags."

HOT SPOTS

Hot spots are areas in your home where any kind of conflict or other behavior problems occur with the most regularity. These could be fights between cats or with other animals, or even attacks on you or visitors. These areas are often created in the social vortex; the area where the most beings intersect is where a conflict over territory can fester. One good way to identify hot spots is to use tape to place an X on the spots where you notice conflicts occurring. Over time, and with accumulating X's, you'll be able to identify patterns that can help you see the problem areas and make the necessary changes.

AMBUSH ZONES AND DEAD ENDS

Ambush zones and dead ends are specific types of hot spots where conflicts are almost inevitable due to their relationship to the space as a whole. These areas are often created (or at the least exacerbated) by furniture placement or architectural elements. For example, if the area where you keep the litter box has only one entrance/exit, and it is placed at the end of a hallway or behind the washing machine, it sets up an ambush zone opportunity where one cat can stand guard outside the entrance, preventing others from coming or going. Ambush zones can be corners or dead ends, as well as spots that are in the center of a room where the overowning cat tries to control the traffic flow. It's important when Catifying to identify and eliminate all ambush zones and dead ends.

Once you identify the problem areas, you can start to look at possible solutions to create a better traffic flow. Here are some tools to consider:

TRAFFIC CIRCLE

Just like a traffic circle works in the real world, a cat traffic circle helps to divert the flow of traffic by circling the traffic around an object, like a cat tree or other piece of furniture, in order to diffuse potential conflict. This is a useful technique to try once you have identified hot spots.

(For an example of a traffic circle in action, see the case study of Thumbelina, Tinkerbell, Tigger, and Sahara on page 261.)

REVOLVING DOOR

The revolving door is a device that helps keep the traffic flowing in an ambush zone or dead end. It is created with some kind of climbing structure, like shelves or a cat tree, that allows the cat to continue moving through the area until they are out of harm's way.

(For an example of a revolving door in action, see the case study of Olive and Pepper on page 104.)

Martin Barraud/OJO Images/Getty Images

ESCAPE ROUTES

When a cat is cornered, he will always look for an escape route, so it's essential to provide these escapes wherever necessary. This goes hand-in-hand with the elimination of dead ends.

(For an example of escape routes in action, see the case study of Darla and Kashmir on page 148.)

CAT GEOMETRY

When a cat enters a room, he immediately evaluates all the angles, dead ends, potential ambush zones, and the traffic flow (as we mention when discussing Cat Chess, page 105). There is usually a pattern to the movements and behaviors of a cat (or cats) in every room; this is cat geometry. By analyzing the angles and mapping these patterns, you can discover environmental solutions to behavioral problems.

The Vertical World

When given the opportunity, cats will inhabit all space—floor to ceiling and everywhere in between. Cats are natural climbers, so it only makes sense that we must consider the vertical world when Catifying. Remember, as we mentioned when discussing Tree Dwellers, the vertical world isn't just way up high; it includes all levels from just off the floor, to chair height, to tabletop, to bookcase, to the highest points in the room.

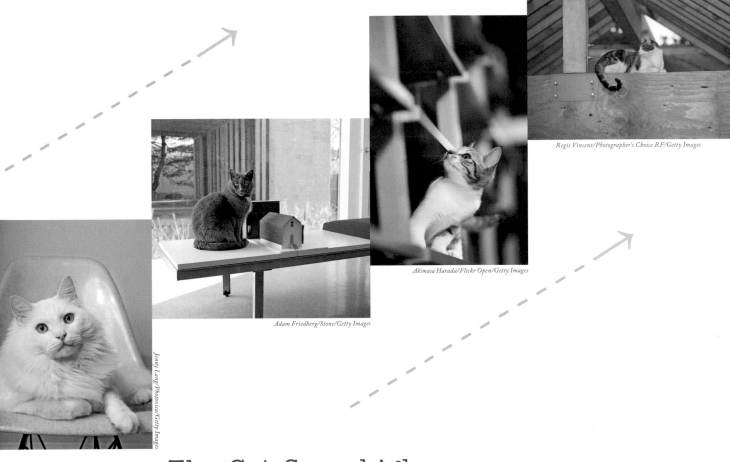

Jenny Lang/Photexia/Getty Images

Adam Friedberg/Stone/Getty Images

Akimasa Harada/Flickr Open/Getty Images

Regis Vincent/Photographer's Choice RF/Getty Images

The Cat Superhighway

This is one of the most important components of Catification. A cat superhighway is a path that allows cats to navigate a room without touching the ground. This is the key to creating good traffic flow and providing your cat with access to the vertical world. A cat superhighway should be the main feature in every Catification plan.

. . .

A good cat superhighway contains the same elements as a good *human* superhighway. Everything revolves around maximun efficiency and minimum chance of collision. Yours should include these features:

MULTIPLE LANES

It's essential to include multiple lanes on your cat superhighway, especially when designing for multiple cats. On a cat superhighway, lanes are not dictated by yellow lines, but rather by the imaginary lines along the vertical axis. Adding lanes allows traffic to flow freely and gives your cat options for exploring the space from different heights.

(For a good example of multiple lanes in action, see the study of Jackson's Catified space on page 85.)

ON/OFF RAMPS

On/off ramps allow your cat to access to the lanes of the superhighway. These are also the escape routes on a cat superhighway. When you're designing, be sure to provide multiple ways for your cat to enter and exit the highway, especially in a multi-cat household.

DESTINATIONS AND REST STOPS

Like any good traffic planner, when looking at your superhighway plan, ask yourself, "Where is this going?" Adding destinations gives your cat a reason to use the highway. The difference between a destination and a rest stop is mainly about where in the room the spot is. For example, placing a cat bed on the top of a bookshelf that's part of your superhighway creates the perfect destination. Small perches placed along the path provide little rest stops where your cat can stop and take in the sights.

Here are some things to watch out for when designing your cat superhighway:

HOT SPOTS, AMBUSH ZONES, AND DEAD ENDS

As in our discussion about urban planning, just because the world is vertical doesn't mean it's free of conflict zones. Keep an eye out for anywhere on the superhighway where flare-ups might occur. Add extra lanes or on/off ramps to eliminate dead ends and keep the traffic moving with momentum.

NARROW LANES

Just like on a real highway, narrow lanes can create bottlenecks, leading to potential conflict. In the world of cat traffic, gridlock equals surefire conflict. Nothing signals a disagreement between cats as surely as the "staredown." When cats freeze and stare at one another, bad things often ensue. Lanes should be wide enough for cats to comfortably walk (at least eight or nine inches deep), and in a multi-cat household, two cats should be able to comfortably pass each other at every point on the highway, or they should have the option to choose an alternative route.

OUT-OF-REACH AREAS

Perhaps the biggest concern when building a cat superhighway is ensuring that every part of the highway is easily accessible in case of emergency. Imagine chasing your cat around with a ladder if you had to evacuate, or even just for a trip to the vet. Be sure there are no parts of the highway you can't access. This will also make cleaning easier.

Territory Markers

The final pieces of good Catification are territory markers. As we learned, cat mojo is all about ownership of territory, and cats need to mark their territory in order to feel confident. They do this in a positive way by leaving their scent and by scratching, which leaves marks that can be seen and smelled by others. Negative marking includes spraying and urinating, and that is what we are trying to avoid by Catifying.

As you review your Catification plan, be sure to include plenty of appropriate territory markers, because if you don't decide what and where they will be, your cat will decide for you, and you might not like his choices! Cats will leave their scent on your regular furniture simply by sitting or sleeping on it. You can also add cat trees, beds, scratching posts, blankets, and toys for your cat to mark and call his own.

SCENT SOAKERS

Items made out of soft materials that will absorb a cat's scent are called scent soakers. Soft beds and blankets, carpeted surfaces, and even cardboard and sisal scratchers allow your cat to rub or scratch and leave his scent behind.

Cat Sundial

Got a cat? Got windows? If you're reading this book, it's a safe bet you have the first, and if you live . . . well, just about anywhere, you have the second. With these two things at the ready, you can practice Sundial Catification!

In our experience, cats by and large follow the sun around the home. You'll most likely see competition for territorial resources around whatever window is letting in the most sun at a particular time of day. With that understanding, the best we can do for our four-legged sun worshippers is give them scent soakers in the spots they covet most. This will allow a sense of ownership over areas that are arguably the most important: next to the couch and your bed. Also, Sundial Catification is a fantastic tool to use in multi-cat households. Having beds, trees, condos, et cetera, placed by sun-facing windows and wherever the sun might land predictably in your home allows cats to practice the secret feline art of time-sharing. You've no doubt seen it in action in your home, as one cat walks up to another sitting in a window or couch seat and gently (or not so gently) says, "Ahem! It is 6:03 a.m. exactly. Time for you to move on!" And usually, that's what happens. Remember, the best medicine for diffusing multi-cat tensions is having enough territorial resources so that the cats don't feel the need to fight over them. Sundial Catification will get you well on the way to that goal.

CATIFICATION DOESN'T END WITH YOUR WALLS

When you're designing for territorial ease, you also should be looking outside the boundaries of your house. Don't forget about what goes on out there. Do you have a backyard? Are there animals in the yard? You might have to diffuse tension from what's going on out there by introducing sight blockers or other environmental elements.

Jackson's Walk-through

We're going to show you the process Jackson uses to evaluate an environment and come up with a Catification plan. You'll need to see how it works so you can evaluate your own home. It's important to take a look around and see what's working and what's not working and use that as the basis of your own Catification plan.

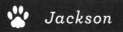 **Jackson**

When I walk into a room, I immediately start scanning. First, I notice how many cats there are. Is there just one, or are we talking about multiple cats? How many? Is there evidence of dogs? Children? Then I start looking, first and foremost, at the natural flow of traffic, at the organic establishment of destinations, hot spots, rest stops, and ambush zones. For example, that table right over there—I see one cat is just sitting there. What is he waiting for? To pounce on that other cat as he comes around the corner? No movement in the world of cats is random, no muscle twitch wasted.

Next comes demilitarization. I'm looking at all of these ambush zones and dead ends that militarize the area, that create a playing field for the expert cat chess champion. Armed with my roll of tape to mark these spots, I'm making a checklist: okay, we have to open this up; we have to block this off. We have to get rid of this under. We have to make sure that we have escape routes all over the place.

While there are no wasted movements in the cat world, there are definitely random moves in the world of humans. Beds, scratchers, blankets, bowls, litter boxes—all of these are potential territory markers—but usually are just thrown wherever. I see every object as a potential scent soaker, territory marker, traffic circle, or revolving door. My job is to create order out of territorial chaos. Maybe there is a scratcher in the room, but is it just sitting there, or is it doing a job? If we have a scratching post right there, why? This is that moment where I hold guardians' feet to the fire; they do what they believe they should by getting condos, scratchers, even more litter boxes, but then place them in a darkened corner? That scratcher should be at the entrance to the room, for instance, and that cat tree next to a window, where the cats can do something with it. It could provide a destination, or an extra lane of traffic to help avoid territorial collisions; it can be a crucial component in an overall scheme, or it could just . . . be there.

Now my attention goes to about four feet off the ground. Now I'm on to the height of tables and chairs and desks, and I'm seeing how the cats can get around. Now I'm starting to think about the cat superhighway. I'm starting to think about how these cats get around this room without touching the floor, if they so desire.

Well, we've got this end table that leads to this chair over here that leads to this dining room table, then to the bookcase and down. Well, you've got that level taken care of. What about above this level? We don't have much there. Here's where we really need to add some things. Now I'm thinking about adding on/off ramps and destinations, dealing with dead ends, et cetera.

Doing this initial scan from floor to ceiling helps me gather everything I need—the flow and the blockages, the relationships and potential skirmishes, and of course the human components—to assess the environment and put together a plan for Catifying.

Catification Nation

While compiling this book, something amazing happened: We invited our followers to submit details on their own Catification projects, and we were instantly flooded with responses from all over the world.

As we sifted through the mountain of cat superhighways, catios, and cocoons, we couldn't help but be struck by the obvious and energizing conclusion: We are part of a global community. We have a flag to fly. We are united by our love for our animal companions and armed with the dedication to enhance territorial mojo for the Raw Cat and provide a safe, comfortable home for the housecat. We are Catification Nation.

PART 2

catification in action

Now that you know about the Raw Cat and have a better understanding of who your cat is, it's time to build an environment that's exciting and fits the Raw Cat's and, more specifically, your cat's, needs. Of course, every environment is unique, and every problem can be solved in multiple ways, so you'll probably have to experiment with different solutions to find just the right thing for your cat and your home.

On the following pages, we've gathered all kinds of example projects, complete with our commentary to help you better understand how each project solves a specific problem. And remember, every one of these projects and examples can be tailored to your style and budget easily. It's your home, too! The goal of Catification is to make everyone happy.

Below are some special features you'll find highlighted throughout this section.

No-Excuses Catification

These are projects for everyone who says, "I don't have the money for a cat tree," or "I'm a disaster with a hammer in my hand." These projects require materials that you likely already have in your home or you can easily grab at your local hardware store, and they can be done by anyone. Stop making excuses, and Catify your world!

Catification Essentials

These are things every Catified home should have. They are basically necessities for living with cats. We find these things used over and over again, and they make life with cats just a little bit easier.

Cat Daddy Dictionary

Look out for Jackson's key terms of Catification, and commit them to memory!

KATE'S PRO TIPS

Kate offers her expertise on how-to projects. Learn from the pro!

MULTI-CAT MOJO

Remember, Catification is for all cat households, whether you have one cat or multiple cats. Many of our examples are geared specifically toward households that have more than one cat, so, if you have only one, you should get another cat! (Hint, hint.)

a super-stylish setup for two raw cats

A Behind-the-Scenes Look at *My Cat from Hell*, Season 5, Episode 1

Darwin and Morello, two Savannah cats, live with their dad, Jacques, in a high-rise overlooking downtown Austin, Texas. Their natural instincts had them climbing the walls and creating a ruckus. Darwin's curiosity often got him into trouble, whereas Morello was truly wild and suspicious of humans; and when she was suspicious, she often became violent. When visitors came over, it was like entering the wild. These cats clearly needed more territory to explore in order to prevent a full-blown attack.

Living with two high-energy cats like Darwin and Morello can be extreme—it definitely calls for extreme Catification. These two cats needed to run and jump, and that's exactly what they were doing—jumping right on to the suspended range hood in the kitchen and almost pulling it out of the ceiling! This created a few challenges. First, we needed to deter the cats from jumping on the range hood; then we needed to create a place where they were allowed to run and jump; and lastly we had to work within Jacques's modern aesthetic.

© Paul Bardagjy

DARWIN YELLING

© 2014 Discovery Communications, LLC

MORELLO HISSING

© 2014 Discovery Communications, LLC

Savannahs are a genetic cross between a domestic housecat and the serval, a medium-size African wildcat. Each purebred Savannah cat has a filial generation number, which refers to how many generations that particular cat is removed from its African serval ancestry. An F1 Savannah cat comes from a first-generation litter and has a serval parent. An F2 comes from a second-generation litter and has a serval grandparent, and so on. Darwin is an F5, and Morello is an F2, meaning she is much closer to her wildcat ancestors than he is.

 Jackson

Here we had two Savannahs: Darwin (an F5) who was more cat than wild, and Morello (an F2) who was much more wild than cat. The Catification process here was going to be about creating an environment that met the needs of both cats halfway. In Darwin's case, it was about dealing with this goofy, high-energy Savannah who loves to do things like jump on the range hood. A cat version of Dennis the Menace, this twenty-pound ball of muscle is always exploring and getting into trouble.

And then there's Morello. I'm not scared of many cats, but I was scared to death of her the first day I met her. Her inclination when she met new people was to be suspicious and fearful, which led her to corner herself, so that she appeared coiled and ready to strike out. In this state, she was fierce, and she scared the hell out of everybody. In her case, we had to cater to the rawest of Raw Cats. Darwin, on the other hand, just needed an outlet for his energy.

I had to call in Kate because I had two Savannahs with very specific needs, but I also had a guardian with a *very* specific design aesthetic who was also *very* nervous about me changing anything in his house. This is the essence of our collaborative effort. As soon as I walked into that condo, I was struck with fear that Jacques would reject anything we did. If Kate couldn't get this guy on board, my only hope for this household would sink.

 Kate

When I first met Jacques, it was clear that he was a big factor in this design—we had to make him happy. He hadn't done much at all environmentally for the cats, so they were just making their own rules. I could also tell from his interactions with the cats that he really loves them, and they have a good relationship, but he never took their needs into consideration when he designed his place, so they were tearing it up out of boredom and frustration.

WILDCAT/DOMESTIC CAT MEETING POINT

We had to cater to both Darwin and Morello, the Raw Cat in each of them having very different needs. Even though they were the same breed, one was very much a domestic cat (Darwin) and the other very much a wildcat (Morello). Morello would never be as comfortable entering the world of humans as Darwin is. We had to make it so that everything served two functions. While we were creating places (other than the range hood) where Darwin could run and jump, that same space up high was going to be a resting/observation post for Morello.

THE RANGE HOOD YES/NO

We needed to make it clear to the cats that the range hood was a big "no"—not a playground, not a lane of traffic, not a destination. With the range hood off-limits, that meant we had to create a superhighway leading Darwin and Morello away from the range hood, giving them appealing destinations and

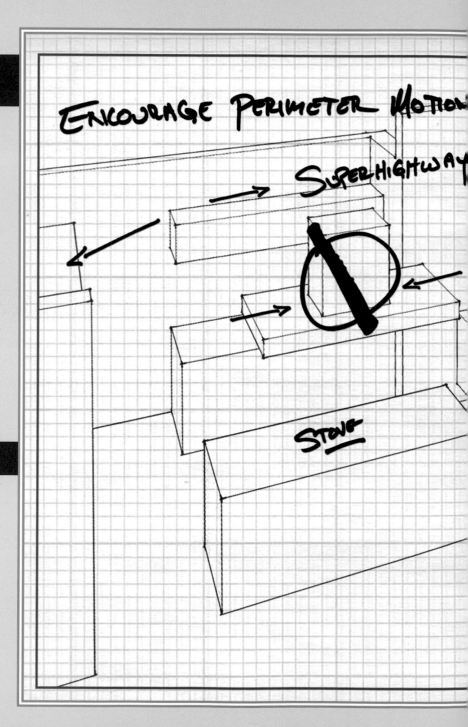

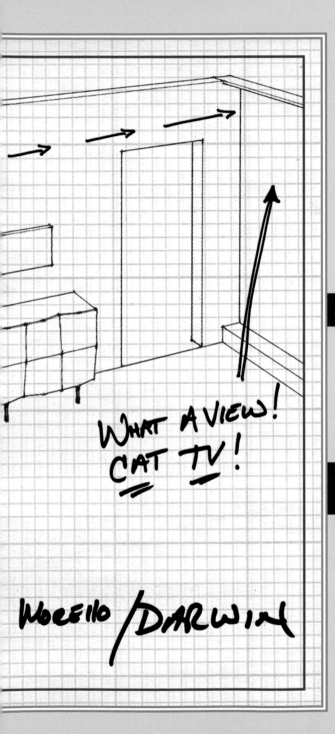

WHAT A VIEW!
CAT TV!

MORELLO / DARWIN

traffic lanes so they wouldn't even be tempted to go near the range hood anymore. We couldn't just say "no," and we couldn't just block it off; we had to give them a "yes," acknowledging that, for the cats, the kitchen is an important social area. The superhighway still gives them access to the kitchen but steers them away from the range hood and connects to other parts of the house as well.

BUILT FOR SPEED

This superhighway had to be designed to take a serious beating, since Darwin and Morello each weighs almost twenty pounds. We had to be sure to securely fasten all the shelves with heavy-duty wall anchors and put something on all the surfaces to prevent slipping.

THE DESIGN-CONSCIOUS GUARDIAN

Of course, all of this had to be done in a way that meshed with Jacques's modern aesthetic. Each feature had to be treated almost like a piece of art, making the Catification fit seamlessly into the interior design; otherwise, Jacques was likely to just tear it all out when we left.

Catification Features

- **Floor-to-ceiling climbing pole** lets the cats climb to the top of the kitchen cabinets.
- **Range hood cover** tells the cats the range hood is off-limits!
- **Kitchen cabinet tops** are integrated into the superhighway.
- **Wraparound cat shelf** extends the super-highway from the cabinet tops to the climbing wall in the dining area.
- **Carpet** on all shelves prevents slipping.
- **Wall-mounted scratchers** create added territorial marking on the climbing wall.
- **Step shelves** lead from the top of the sideboard to the shelves above, creating an alternate on/off ramp.

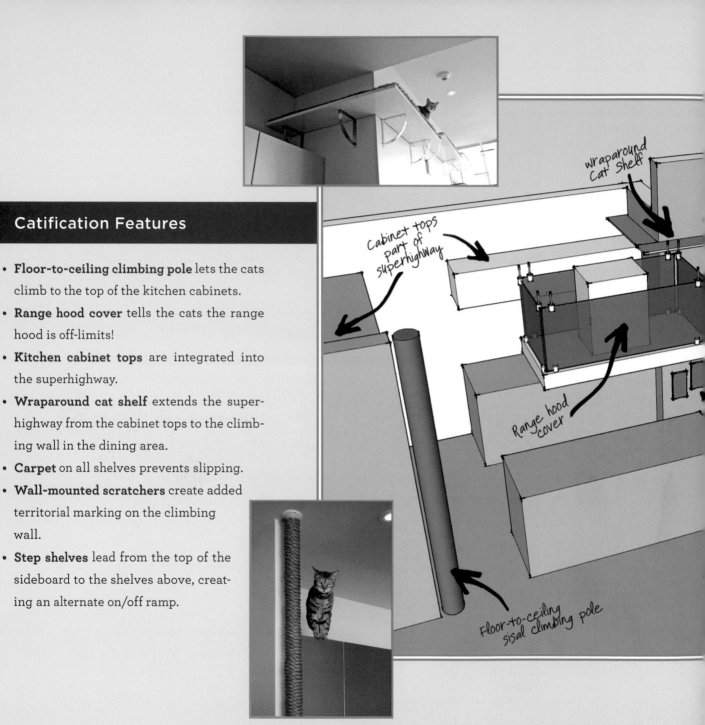

wraparound cat shelf

cabinet tops part of superhighway

Range hood cover

Floor-to-ceiling sisal climbing pole

Carpet

step shelves

Nonslip mat

Wall-mounted scratchers

Tension pole cat tree

- **Nonslip mat** on the top of the sideboard prevents slipping and protects the surface from scratches. The sideboard is integrated into the superhighway, so clear the clutter!
- **Tension pole cat tree** in the window completes the superhighway, allowing easy entrance and exit. Carpet on the steps prevents slipping.

KATE'S PRO TIPS

Wraparound Cat Shelf

- -

To make a shelf that wraps around a corner, you could cut an L shape out of a piece of plywood, but the easiest way is to use two straight shelves or boards and butt them up against each other to create the L shape. Use two flat brackets to secure the shelves together for added stability.

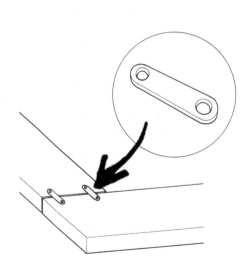

MAKING THE RANGE HOOD COVER

The range hood portion of this project is a classic example of the "Yes/No"—deterring cats from unwanted areas or behaviors while giving them an appropriate alternative. We needed to make it clear that the range hood was a big "no." If the cats continued to jump onto the range hood, the whole thing could potentially tear out of the ceiling and come crashing down. Our solution was to block off access to the range hood, but it had to be done in a way that worked with the décor. Here's how we did it.

MATERIALS AND TOOLS

Translucent acrylic sheets, ceiling-mounted cable sign hanging hardware (available from signage or display supply companies), double-sided tape, and electric drill/driver.

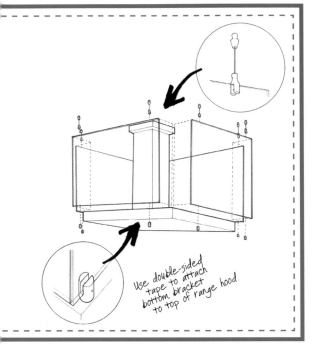

Use double-sided tape to attach bottom bracket to top of range hood.

First we measured the length and width of the range hood and calculated the size of the acrylic panels we needed. We left about six inches between the tops of the panels and the ceiling. Initially, we thought of using art on the panels, but we were concerned it wouldn't gel with Jacques's taste in art—plus we were worried that by using opaque panels, it would close off the space above the range hood, creating a claustrophobic feeling. Instead, we chose translucent orange acrylic for the panels, which adds a splash of color to the room and coordinates with the existing color palette.

The panels were suspended from the ceiling using a cable hanging system made for display signs. It's quite easy to install: Simply attach one fixture to the ceiling after measuring to find the proper placement and then attach the other fixture to the acrylic panel. In this case, we used a third fixture to hold the bottom of the panel to the top of the range hood surface using double-sided tape.

BEFORE: CATS LAUNCHING ONTO THE RANGE HOOD

The colored acrylic serves as a visual and physical barrier for the cats, letting them know the area is off-limits. The translucent panels still allow for light to come through, keeping the open, airy feeling in the space. Actually, the end result looks like a piece of suspended art after all.

AFTER: RANGE HOOD IS BLOCKED OFF

DARWIN READY TO LAUNCH, BUT CLEARLY GETTING THE MESSAGE THAT THE RANGE HOOD IS NOW OFF-LIMITS

catification

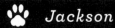

Kate, what part of this project were you the most proud of?

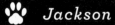

I think seeing Darwin and Morello up on those shelves, instantly, the second we showed them the design, was probably the most rewarding part. I love the range hood cover, too. I think it's a really beautiful solution to the problem; it worked—no more twenty-pound cats crashing onto the range hood—and it looks great. That was the "no," and it works hand-in-hand with the "yes." The cats were so comfortable on the shelves, up on the high levels, climbing down the tree, using all the different on and off ramps. I think it was incredibly successful because of how it was received by both the cats and by Jacques.

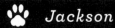

There were many successes in this case. Jacques was happy, and Darwin wasn't crashing into the range hood anymore, but for me, the most important aspect was Morello being able to explore her world. I was stunned when I saw Morello up on the shelves. I mean, talk about the toughest critic in the room. When it comes to cats, the ones baring the most teeth are the biggest critics. On

the final day, her reaction was saying, "Thanks, I needed this!" It was more about necessity than comfort. A cat like Morello needs Catification. Without it, not only is she unhappy, but people are in danger.

On my last visit, I gave Morello a treat while she was up on top of the cabinet. She took the treat from my hand and walked away. Believe it or not, that was a huge moment. This is as close as anyone besides Jacques gets to interacting with Morello. I said to her, "I tried to treat you like something you're not: a domestic housecat. This new superhighway allows you to be who you are—a true, raw Tree Dweller, a cat who only finds safety and confidence at arm's length from most people." This Catification felt like a major accomplishment because on the prior visit, Morello was trying to take my arm off because she was so scared of being on the floor, and now she had the environment that she needed to be herself.

In the coming pages, we will be highlighting several projects submitted by members of the Catification Nation community. These are meant to serve as examples of what's possible. We want you to be inspired by what these creative cat guardians have done and learn from their wisdom, but not be intimidated. With that in mind, here are some themes we noticed in many of the projects that might help you:

- **Don't get overwhelmed!** Concentrate on building the framework first and try not to get hung up on "the little things." You can always add on later. You'll be amazed at how many more possibilities you'll see after the first phase is done. One of the beautiful things about Catification is that the canvas is never finished; there's always something else you can add.
- **Good Catification designs are scalable;** they can be expanded and adapted over time as individual cats grow and mature and as cats join and leave your home. A scalable design accommodates these changes.
- **Think outside the box!** We love the "hack" projects where cat guardians take something that wasn't originally designed for cat use and repurpose it to make a completely original design that is exactly what the cat(s) needed.

Remember, what works for someone else and their cats won't necessarily work for your home, but there might be one element in their project that sparks your imagination. Just take what you need and leave the rest!

SUBMITTED BY:
Rebecca and
Richard Brittain,
Clearwater, Florida

CATS:
Emily and Kirby

a place to perch

A CAT TREE INSPIRED BY NATURE

EMILY

The nature-inspired cat tree came about when my "clients" Emily and Kirby moved with us to our new house and realized it did not come furnished with anything at all like their beloved "long, tall wall shelf thingy" from the old house, which they had used to climb, sleep, and play on ALL THE TIME. They were already a little peeved because we had so rudely removed it when we listed the house for sale.

At the new house, the cats were spending the whole day sleeping, lounging, and eating in a back office room where we were working, and not leaving to get exercise or explore—which we, as their designers/guardians, wanted to remedy.

KIRBY

Since we were planning to start using a larger, brighter, more central room of the new house for our office, we definitely wanted to integrate the cats' needs into that new space. Emily said she didn't really care WHAT it looked like, as long as it was comfy, easy for her to climb, and "near where you work during the day so I can get lots of snuggles." Kirby blinked and agreed that yes, he MIGHT be getting a little tubbier from lack of exercise, and would at least THINK about using the cat tree.

Materials and Budget

We used $100 in driftwood from a seller on craigslist and recycled three platforms and some sisal rope from the cats' old cat tower. Fluffy bathroom rugs ($24 total) cover the landings and can be taken off and shaken out.

We used lag bolts to attach the driftwood to the ceiling, walls, and other pieces. Richard predrilled holes and then attached the lag bolts into wall or ceiling studs. The holes

are counter sunk so we can fill in with wood plugs to hide the bolt heads. (Haven't done that yet!)

The piece at the ceiling was wrapped in a heavy-duty strip of metal; then the bolt was drilled through that and the wood, into the ceiling. We wrapped the metal strip with sisal to hide it.

The spiral steps started out as short, round logs of driftwood. Richard split each one, and we placed them in the correct stepping positions before drilling and bolting them to the central post and wall. The tools used were a drill with various bits, a chainsaw, and a table saw.

Rebecca and Richard's Tips

We started with the large ceiling piece of driftwood, then slowly, over a few nights, pieced the rest together, cutting and sawing the driftwood as needed to fit the wall and space. Richard thankfully is very handy with tools (and he's very patient).

The Result

It's been finished for only about a week. Emily is the more outgoing of the two, and she's already figured out the steps and uses the first platform for naps. Kirby is more cautious and hasn't yet climbed it on his own, but he loves the sisal scratcher at the bottom. We built it knowing they may or may not take to it, but both already spend more time out in the space, playing and hanging out in the area (with me at the computer during the day), so we consider that a success!

This is a winner on so many levels! It's not only a great example of sharing space with cats, but it's one where you don't know where the cat tree ends and your furniture begins, in a beautifully integrated way—and not in a "crazy cat lady house" kind of way. Actually, if you took the cats away, it looks like a stunning human design choice. That is the true nature of Catification. I would be proud to have that wall be part of my house.

I would love to see a bridge from cat world to human world, continuing the highway from the top of the tree to the top of the bookshelf. I'd also like to see another exit point on the left side of the bookcase. This would complete the superhighway by allowing for better traffic flow.

🐾 *Kate*

I know this looks like an elaborate design, and you might be thinking, *I could never do that*! But hold on—it's not that complicated. This project uses simple, natural materials and basic construction techniques. With some careful planning and sturdy mounting hardware, you can easily build a cat tree like this, even if you're not a master carpenter!

When making your Catification plan, imagine it without any cats and ask yourself, is this something I would still have in my home even if I didn't have cats?

cat daddy's lair

A PEEK INSIDE JACKSON'S PAD

Here's a peek at the Catification we did for Jackson's own home when he was living in Los Angeles with his three cats, Velouria, Chuppy, and Caroline, plus his little dog, Rudy. Jackson threw out an SOS the second he moved into this tiny, 500-square-foot guest house—he knew this would be a Catification challenge.

🐾 *Jackson*

I walked into this space and immediately panicked. My cats have extremely big personal space bubbles and needed enough room to get away from each other. My dog, Rudy, a blind Jack Russell–Beagle mix, explored the world (including all cats) with her nose and mouth. Not a good mix in 500 square feet. The idea here was to make sure that all three cats could stay out of one another's hair and definitely out of Rudy's mouth. Hello, Kate, can you help?!

🐾 *Kate*

Yes, because the space was so small, we definitely had challenges in accommodating all the animals' needs, but we also had to define spaces for Jackson to do what he needed. He had to live there, too, after all. We had to be really creative when we were putting together the Catification features along with the human features.

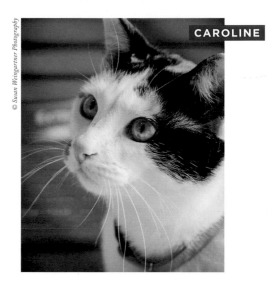

CAROLINE

CHUPPY

VELOURIA

RUDY

🐾 *Jackson*

When we were designing this space, we really took into consideration the very different needs of these animals. At the time, Velouria was around twenty years old, Chuppy was nineteen, and Caroline was three. Caroline was a former feral who was always looking to disappear either way up or way down. She exercised her feral muscles in whatever cracks and crevices she could find; whether down on the floor or up in the ceiling, she was constantly looking to hide. Velouria, in her heyday, would often jump from the floor to the top of the door in a single bound. Even at twenty years old, she was still always looking for up, always looking to explore the vertical world, as opposed to Caroline,

who just wanted to hide. And then we had Chuppy, who became very arthritic in her older years and never liked other cats in her face to begin with. However, Chuppy got along really well with Rudy, the blind dog who explored the world with her nose and mouth.

So with these characters in mind, we had to build all these lanes of traffic: one lane for Caroline where we had to block off the highs and lows, gentle inclines for Chuppy whose arthritis had to be accounted for, and enough safe exploration space for twenty-year-old Velouria, who didn't know her own age-related limitations. And, oh yeah, Rudy.

Jackson's Superhighway

The top priority was to create a cat superhighway throughout the house. Remember, on any good superhighway, you need to have ample lanes to accommodate the flow of traffic, as well as on/off ramps. In a multi-cat household, sharing a lane of traffic can cause conflict. Cats shouldn't have to compete for space on a one-lane dirt road. When two cars are driving toward each other on a single-lane road, someone is going to have to pull over to let the other pass. Although human drivers might have roadside etiquette, cats rarely do. When two cats go head on, the feline version of honking your horn involves teeth and claws. To avoid this, you have to create a cat superhighway with multiple lanes. As you add cats to your home, you have to start thinking about urban planning, like you would in any growing city. If you go from having one cat to having two, you need to expand.

INTEGRATING CAT AND HUMAN NEEDS

What people might not notice when they look at this project is that there are actually four lanes of traffic—the floor, the sofa and ottoman, and two levels of shelves. All these lanes incorporate both animal use and human use; for instance, the desk is for Jackson to work at, but it's also incorporated into the superhighway. The credenza holds the TV as well as the cats' elevated feeding area. The sofa and furniture are part of the superhighway, too. Your cats are probably going to use your human furniture as a lane of traffic, whether you build it that way or not, so why not plan for it? It does no good to provide your cat with a windowsill that clearly leads to the mantle but then consider the mantle off-limits.

DESKTOP LANDING PAD

In the office nook, we watched the cats' behavior and found that they were using the desk surface as part of the highway, moving from the middle window shelf to the shelf above the desk by jumping on and off the desk. Along with being inconvenient, it was also dangerous for the cats to jump from a height onto a laminate surface they couldn't grip. Instead of discouraging this, we accommodated the cats by placing sisal pieces with non-slip backing on the corners of the slippery desk surface.

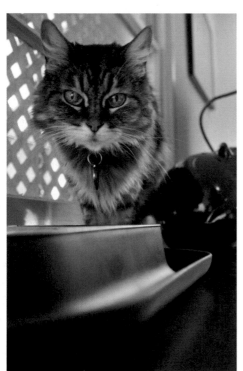

SPLIT-LEVEL DINING

As anyone who lives with both dogs and cats knows, sometimes it's necessary to separate them at feeding time. (Greedy dogs!) In order to address this issue, we decided to use the top of the low bookshelf in the living room for the cats' feeding station. To make

it easier for the older cats to reach the raised surface, we added a set of modern pet stairs. The cats were able to easily access their food while Rudy dined on the lower level.

We continued the highway in the bedroom with more shelves leading from a low table up to the top of the dresser. Strategically placed cat beds and scratch lounges made for nice destinations along the highway where happy cats could stop for a nap.

 Jackson

I think one of the most wonderful elements of this particular cat super-highway is that it was difficult to assess the needs of our cat clients. Given a brand-new space, how would they decide to timeshare? Since the space was so much smaller than their previous territory, who would try to dominate certain

areas, and who would find confidence and safety in various levels of the vertical world?

Kate and I embraced the challenge. We built a highway with four vertical lanes so the three cats could all explore different heights in their own time. The configuration also allowed me to get further into the mojo of each of my cats.

For instance, I discovered that when given access to "trees," "bushes," and "caves," Caroline would choose the latter, allowing her feral nature to take over, attempting to "disappear" herself from human view. The last thing one wants when constructing a cat super-highway is to encourage a fearful mind-set. I wound up having to block off the top of a closet I thought would be a great private zone, initially lined with cat beds, as well as underneath virtually any piece of furniture. Her challenge line became living on very midrange heights like the bed, the arms of the couch, etc. Cat beds were then placed strategically in those areas.

The point is that we provided an incredibly flexible skeleton, one which we could change with the emerging individual and communal needs of my three cats. It goes to show you that Catification is a journey, not a destination; the space as well as the process need to be given the room to breathe as the inhabitants cross their challenge lines and become more and more confident.

SUBMITTED BY:
Sara and Erik;
Minneapolis, Minnesota

CATS:
Whisper, Weasley, Wobbly,
Waffles, and Millie

operation: catify your living room!

A HIGH-UP HANGOUT SPOT

There's an odd space way up high in our living room that gets wonderful morning light and is a perfect place for cats to hang out, but there was no way for the cats to access it. When we moved into the house, we initially put houseplants in the nook to keep them safe from nibbling cats, but it was very inconvenient to care for them by ladder. We always wanted to make a kitty clubhouse up there to give the cats a place to observe from above, to enjoy the sunlight, and to remove themselves from ground-level traffic.

When Erik made the first cat tree, the cats immediately took to climbing the tree and using the clubhouse. They enjoyed chasing each other up and down the tree, sleeping in the sun, or just watching household activity from above. They also enjoyed the tree branch bark and used it as a scratching post.

Materials and Budget

We tackled our Catification in three stages. Here's how we did it:

Stage 1: Initial Cat Tree Leading to Nook

- Large burr oak tree branch from ground of local woods (free)
- Oak boards that Erik milled himself from trees felled during a Department of Transportation highway project (free)
- One large bolt from local hardware store (under $5)
- Teak oil, local hardware store, full bottle (under $15)
- Various cat beds and cushions of various ages (ranging from $15 to $30)

We remodeled our entire living room and decided to make sure the design was cat-friendly, cat-practical, and cat-attractive.

Stage 2: Living Room Remodel and Extended Catification

- We replaced all carpet in the house with hardwood floors that Erik milled from "rescued" oak wood.
- We replaced our wood-burning fireplace with a gas insert and designed the new one to be safe for cats and not quite accessible for climbing.
- We reupholstered furniture with easy-to-clean microfiber with no texture (and thus not attractive as a scratching post).
- We added an entertainment center/display case that could be positioned together with the cat tree to add a high, horizontal dimension to accessing the clubhouse.
- Kind friends gave us the Cat Clouds Cat Shelf, which fit in perfectly with our vertical and horizontal design.
- We added sleeping baskets bought at a Goodwill store for less than $5 each on either side of the entertainment center.

- We placed a carpeted cat tree that we have had for years in a new position in the living room for additional medium-level vertical space and outdoor views for the cats.

Stage 3: Continuing Catification (It's an ongoing process!)

- We added a pod bed to the nook. These usually retail for around $100, but we waited until we found a half-price deal.

- Erik designed and built kitty- and fish-shaped window cat perches made from "rescued" oak and walnut, which we attached to our large living room windows overlooking the woods and a creek and lots of interesting wildlife to entertain the cats.
- Erik designed and built tricolored wood (oak, walnut, and cherry) "cat baskets," which the cats love to sit in.

Sara and Erik's Tips

- Check with your spouse/housemate for input on placement of major structural additions to your home! The placement of the first climbing tree was quite impractical because it was so close to the front door and the coat closet—something we use a lot in Minnesota during the winter.

- There are a lot of beautiful Catification products available—but you can also make very attractive cat features with some basic skills and affordable materials. You don't have to be a skilled woodworker (like Erik) to make your house a cat haven. Use your imagination and have fun. Just be sure to thoroughly cat-safety check before letting your cats enjoy it.

- Test out your ideas and plans with your cats before you invest time and money to install everything. For example, before building the cat tree in our living room, we brought in logs and other branches to see how the cats reacted to the texture, smell, etc. They liked the wood, so the project got a green light. On the other hand, Erik just designed a really attractive and unique scratching post prototype. The cats, however, ignore it completely, so we are observing a bit longer and then will go back to the drawing board if they don't show any interest.

- Divide your project into stages to make it more doable if you are feeling challenged by time, budget, or know-how limitations. Our living room Catification evolved over four years, and we add to it periodically when we have new ideas, time, and funds.

The Result

The cats use the Catification features in our living room daily. Our cats are very social with us and with each other, and there are frequently a couple in the "clubhouse" throughout the day and night; when sun is pouring in, they have a slumber party! When we are in the living room, it doesn't take long before the entire crew joins us. There are a lot of options for lounging. We find cats sleeping on our laps, nestled in the pod bed in the clubhouse, draped over the tree branch, or curled up in a basket.

The project has definitely been a hit with the cats, we love seeing them enjoy it, and our friends find the design fun and attractive, too. We are always in "continuous improvement" mode and make modifications as needed. As some of our cats move into their senior years, we will make accommodations for any physical challenges they develop.

Jackson

First of all, props to Sara and Erik for really doing their Catification homework and looking at the world through both their eyes and their cats' eyes at the same time and asking, "How do we make this work for everybody?" They did an awesome job bringing nature into their home and combining the cats' aesthetic with their own. The only thing I would say is keep going, you're not done yet! The superhighway ends at the nook, and if there is an argument between cats up there, it could end badly. I'd encourage them to create another exit from the nook, extending past the front door and down. Allow that superhighway to continue; I don't want to see any trouble in that dead end. Otherwise, this is absolutely an amazing example for all the Catification rookies out there. Great job!

Kate

This is such a terrific showcase for Erik's amazing woodworking skills, but don't be intimidated if you're not as skilled—be inspired! Using a natural tree trunk is a great way to get started, and the cats will love it, too. Be sure to check it carefully for hidden bugs so you don't bring any unwanted critters into your home. I love how they used a smaller piece of the tree to continue the theme across the top of the cabinet. There are so many creative ways you could continue this idea throughout the house.

finding the perfect cat bed

Countless styles of cat beds are available, and there's one to match every style and every budget. Cat beds are the ultimate scent soaker because beds are territorially significant spots. They also make great destinations and rest stops along your cat superhighway.

Each cat prefers a different type of bed, so you might need to experiment to see which style your cat likes. In addition to finding the type of bed your cat favors, also try out different places throughout your home to find your cat's "confident where" for resting. Some cat beds are really inexpensive, so get several of them, toss them everywhere, and watch to see where your cat prefers to rest.

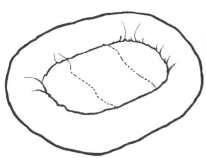

Here are a few common types of cat beds to try:

Donut beds are usually oval and flat with a slightly raised edge, just enough for cats to rest against but keeping them mostly out in the open.

Bucket beds have taller sides, making for a nice, deep spot cats can sit down in and peek out over the edge.

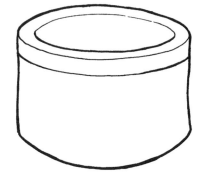

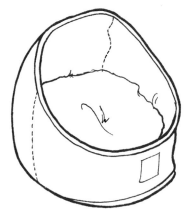

Hooded beds create more of a burrow in which cats can nestle and be partially covered.

Pod beds are almost completely enclosed, creating a cocoon. Be sure your pod bed has two openings so no one can get trapped inside.

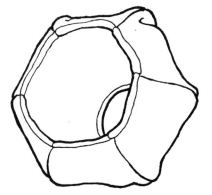

bending the rules of cat chess

A Behind-the-Scenes Look at *My Cat from Hell*, Season 3, Episode 1

Mike and Emilie's small New York City apartment had become a war ground for their two cats, Olive and Pepper. The cats couldn't be left alone in the same room without a terrible fight breaking out. The couple had also been sleeping in separate rooms every night to keep the peace and assuage their guilt of banishing one of the cats from the master bedroom. With their wedding fast approaching, something had to change if Mike and Emilie ever hoped to go on a worry-free honeymoon.

Olive never took her eyes off Pepper. "General Olive" was a master at cat chess, cutting off Pepper's every move, and Pepper immediately became the Wallflower Cat as

soon as she realized she was in Olive's sights. The landscape of the apartment was making the situation far worse, creating ambush zones where Olive could corner Pepper, leaving her with no escape routes. We had to short-circuit the game of cat chess going on here in order to get these two cats to live together peacefully.

CAT DADDY DICTIONARY

CAT CHESS

Cat chess is another way of looking at the "game" of cat and mouse or the "game" of predator and prey. When a hunter is hunting, he surveys his field of vision as if it were a chessboard, ready to go in for a "capture" the moment he sees an opportunity. Great hunters (as most cats are) plot out the next four moves, cutting off angles or escape routes and predicting every move their prey can make.

I remember when we first got to Mike and Emilie's, we walked in and saw what we had to work with, then we just kind of stood there with our mouths open, trying to figure out what to do. So many dead ends and ambush zones everywhere. It was a classic New York City apartment with hallways shaped like a Z, and the problem wasn't just the place, it was also about the players. Olive, obviously being a cat chess champion, meant we needed a strategy for changing up the game.

Kate

Yeah, you just kept looking at the corner in the kitchen where it was obvious Pepper could easily get trapped, and you kept saying, "Up and out, up and out, we've got to get her up and out." There was a rolled-up carpet in

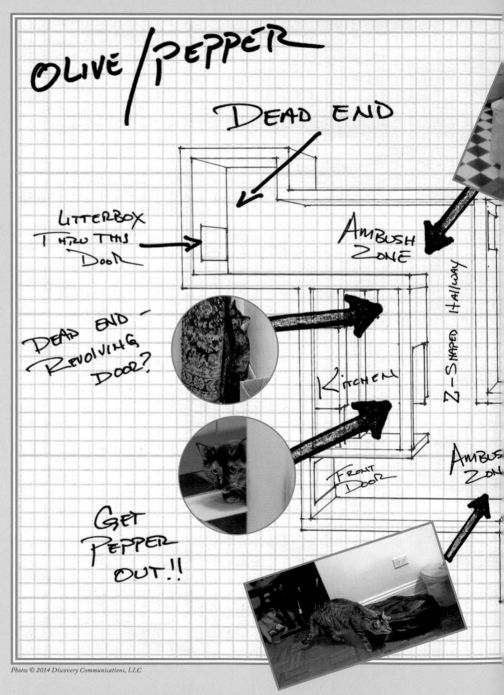

Photos © 2014 Discovery Communications, LLC

the corner creating a terrible dead end. I asked Mike how long the carpet had been there, and he said since they'd moved in, which told me they didn't really need that space, so it gave me an idea that we could do something in that corner.

🐾 *Jackson*

As I was talking about "up and out," it hit me! It had to be like a revolving door, where Pepper runs in to the corner and before she knows it, she's out again. Like in Tai Chi, we needed to use Pepper's flight instinct and natural momentum and reroute her so she'd move through the space and out again the way she came. The concept of momentum is key here. We couldn't let her stop because if she stops, then she freezes; if she freezes, there's a stare down; if there's a stare down, General Olive wins. Because then it's checkmate.

MAKE LIVINGROOM + WINDOW MORE OF AN ATTRACTION

BEDROOM

LIVING ROOM

GENERAL OLIVE'S STANDOFF

Olive started each attack across the room from Pepper, sizing up the entire chessboard, angles of attack, and possible escape routes. She would then make eye contact with Pepper, who would instantly freeze like a deer caught in the headlights, and then Olive would stalk her, expertly cutting off her escape routes, creeping closer and closer until BAM! Full-on attack! This is how cats stalk and kill their prey in the wild, but it's not something anyone wants to live with. Mike and Emilie were constantly on edge, spending way too much time monitoring the cats and trying to keep them separated.

THE VORTEX OF UGLY

The narrow, twisting hallway—typical of New York City apartments—created the perfect ambush zone where Olive frequently trapped Pepper by cutting off her escape routes. Contained in this zone was the bathroom (which housed the litter box) and the couple's bedroom (the most socially

important spot in the house). When this becomes the primary area where warring cats spend their time, there are bound to be conflicts.

PEPPER'S REVOLVING DOOR

Olive would set up camp outside the kitchen, trapping Pepper inside, leaving Pepper with nowhere to go. We tackled this challenge first. We needed to create a "revolving door" in the kitchen that would allow Pepper to get up and out of harm's way. Because Mike and Emilie rent their apartment, we had to come up with a solution that didn't involve drilling into the walls so we used a tension pole climbing tree to create a space-saving vertical environment that didn't require hanging anything from the walls. The tree fits perfectly in the corner, and now if Olive chases Pepper into the kitchen, Pepper automatically goes up the tree in a spiral direction and then she gets spun around and shoots out onto the new shelf we put next to the cat tree and then over onto the newly decluttered countertop. We made sure to add nonslip sisal mats to the top of the new shelf and the counter to give Pepper extra traction.

USE THIS . . .

TO GET FROM THIS . . .

TO THIS.

ALTERNATE ESCAPE ROUTES

To create an alternate escape route in the kitchen, we added a sisal mat to the top of the refrigerator, which is an easy jump from the upper shelves on the tree. Pepper can now escape to a cozy bed on top of the kitchen cabinets, or she can jump down onto the counter (landing on another sisal mat), and head out the other way.

Pepper took immediately to her new climbing

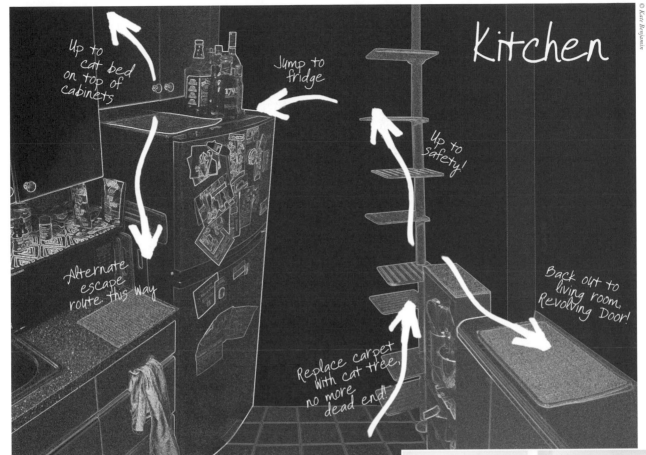

Kitchen

Up to cat bed on top of cabinets

Jump to fridge

Up to safety!

Alternate escape route, this way

Back out to living room, Revolving Door!

Replace carpet with cat tree, no more dead end!

© Kate Benjamin

© Kate Benjamin

© Kate Benjamin

bending the rules of cat chess 111

tree, and Mike and Emilie were thrilled to see their little tortie feeling more relaxed and comfortable. You can see from Pepper's posture that she is feeling less threatened and more confident in her environment. Now, instead of being cornered in the kitchen, Pepper can climb up her cat tree to safety and then exit either to the counter or to the top of the refrigerator.

Mike and Emilie's hallway was another huge issue. The nook in the hallway was a great example of an underused space that, because of a lack of consideration, was creating a problem area for multiple cats. It created another dead end where Olive could corner Pepper for checkmate. To address the dead end, we created another revolving door using Pepper's momentum to spin her around and move her through the space. We actually used two trees that create a whole jungle gym where Pepper can climb up and out of the way. To complete the revolving door in the hallway, we added a small table across the hall with another sisal mat on top. Now Pepper can jump from the tree to the top of the table, allowing her to head back down the hall, instead of being trapped in the alcove.

Once some thought was given to the design and use of the space, the problem was solved, and the cats now have a fabulous new environment to explore and enjoy.

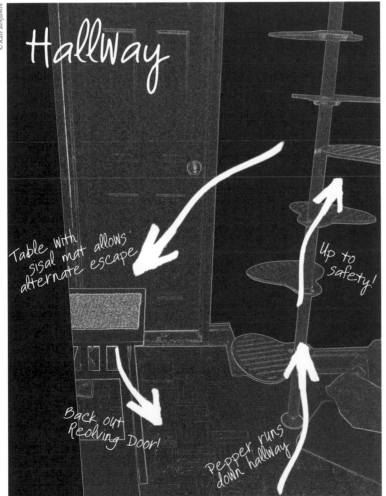

HallWay

Table with sisal mat allows alternate escape

Back out Revolving Door!

Pepper runs down hallway

Up to safety!

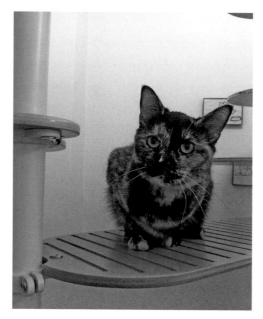

🐾 REVOLVING DOOR 🐾

The revolving door is a device that helps keep the traffic flowing in an ambush zone or dead end. It is created with some kind of climbing structure, like shelves or a cat tree, that allows the cat to continue moving through the area until they are out of harm's way.

No-Excuses Catification:
Clear the Clutter!

You don't always have to add something new just for the cats. Instead, take a look around your home and see if you can designate any surfaces as "cat only" surfaces. Simply clear the clutter and let Kitty know she's welcome on the new surface. That's exactly what we did in the kitchen by clearing the countertop and adding sisal mats with nonslip backing to the top of the shelf next to the tree and the counter. We did the same with the top of the refrigerator and the countertop next to it. Of course, if you don't want your cats on specific surfaces, like the kitchen counter, you'll need to give them other options where they are allowed to go.

SUBMITTED BY:
Rin Krak;
Mertzig, Luxembourg

CATS:
Po and Cookie

a stairway to heaven (cat style)

SPIRAL CAT STAIRS

Because my two cats like to be in high places, I designed and made some cat stairs so they could use the space on top of the cupboard. The use of spiral stairs allowed me to use as little space as possible.

 Jackson

I wanted to highlight this project because it shows the level of attention to detail that you can put into each component of your Catification project. In this case, Rin put everything he had into this spiral staircase, and the results are both beautiful and functional.

I find this project really exciting because there are so many places you can go with it beyond just the top of the cabinet—there's so much potential to create an amazing superhighway that carries over on to the other side of the cupboard. But even just as it is, it's a stunning individual piece.

Materials and Budget

The stairs are made of pine, and the spindle is a copper tube 22 millimeters in diameter. I used a copper tube 15 millimeters in diameter to attach to the ceiling. This tube fits inside the larger one. I did not paint the stairs, because I like the natural look of the wood. I spent about 50€ ($67) for the wood, copper tubes, and some other

materials. I also made a small ledge on the side of the top shelf to prevent the cats from falling down out of the "pirate's nest" when sleeping there.

Rin's Tips

This is an easy-to-build design; it just takes time. There are a lot of steps, about one hundred. It's important to take your time and drill the holes nice and straight. It's not that hard, just start building and take your time. If you are thinking of making something like this, but taller, you could add a support in the middle of the stairs and mount it to the wall for extra support.

🐾 Jackson

Hey folks, don't be intimidated by this! This is an example of somebody using their specific talents and putting them to use for their cats. Find your own specialty, and play to your strengths.

🐾 Kate

Spiral stairs are a great space-saving solution, and the form looks like a beautiful modern sculpture. You could use different natural woods or wood stains or even paint the steps to add a splash of color to your Catification project.

The Result

At first the cats just explored the new stairs, but it didn't take that long before they started to use them. Po loves to lie down in the pirate's nest, and they both use the stairs to get away and lie down and rest on top of the cupboard. I think it is a success for the cats, and it even looks nice.

Catification Essentials

If you decide to give your cats access to a nice piece of furniture—like a coffee table or dresser—it's a good idea to have a piece of tempered glass cut to cover the top surface. This prevents scratches and makes it very easy to clean.

    Remember, if it's a surface that your cats are going to jump onto, be sure to add a nonslip mat so they can grip and not slide off.

SUBMITTED BY:
Nico and Katu;
Bogotá, Colombia

CAT:
Arana

arana's inside playground

A SMALL APARTMENT WITH LOTS OF ROOM TO RUN, JUMP, AND HIDE

We found Arana on the street, and we planned to find another home for her because we didn't have much space in our apartment for her to climb, run, play, or hide. We fell so in love with Arana that—inspired by a few episodes of Jackson Galaxy's show!—we decided to keep her and build her a place of her own inside where she could exercise and play.

Arana was very active from the moment she arrived at our home, and it was clear we needed to create more space for her to jump and run around in. We also knew she wanted to be close to us, so that's why we decided to put her playground in our room.

Our true inspiration was the love we have for Arana. We wanted to keep her in our house but with the best possible conditions, in a safe and very fun place for her to feel loved and happy. We guess what she told us was, "Please! I want to stay with you!"

I absolutely love this. Every picture here speaks of their love for this cat. It's not just "Oh, let's throw up some shelves"; this is about thinking—in a very artistic sense—about what your cat will look like when she's climbing. This project's success allows the guardians to become an audience of sorts; as they move through their environment, our cats show themselves to be choreographers and dancers at the same time. It straddles the line between form and function; it's very aestheti-

cally pleasing to look at, but much of the art here is in how the piece appears with the cat moving through the space. It has a very beautiful sense of flow.

As with many of the Catification projects we see, there is always room for improvement or expansion. In this case, my first thought was, why are there boxes on only one side? There's an opportunity here to have an A, B, and C point in the room; there's the whole area off to the right that has so much potential, but it's empty. I would love to see a continuation of the playground across the whole wall.

I love the suspended boxes that give Arana the perfect tree-dwelling hideaway for surveying her territory. Also the bridge walkways add a unique element to the climbing wall. But my favorite details are the cutouts in the shelves providing an alternate way to get from level A to level B.

Materials and Budget

This was not an expensive project; overall we spent around a hundred dollars. We bought wood from a local store, and the accessories—like screws, wood sealant, shelf brackets, flat braces, rivets, and a PVC tube—from a warehouse store.

Nico's Tips

The trick for successful construction is having a clear idea of the design before you start.

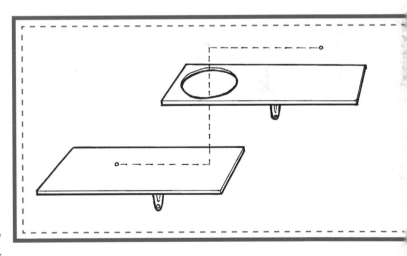

The Result

At first Arana didn't pay much attention to the playground. It was a strange thing for her, and she wouldn't go near it, but with a little bit of patience and some food to encourage her, Arana quickly figured out that it was her own special place. Now she uses her playground every single day. She really loves it because she can completely be herself up there. She runs and jumps and uses all the elements that we have added to the wall. If someday we notice that she stops using something, we will change it so she can continue enjoying it.

catification

operation: catify kate's office!

 Kate

Here's a peek at some Catification I did in my own office. When I originally moved into my condo and set up the office, I made the cabinets over the desk off-limits. At first I thought I was going to display breakable things up there, but I never got around to it. The cats would sit on the desk and look up longingly at the forbidden zone, but I never let them go up because it was just a little too risky letting them jump from the desk all the way up to the top of the cabinets. Finally, one day I gave in and realized that I was never going to put anything up there (I'd just have to dust it anyway!) so I might as well turn that space over to the cats. But I had to give them a better way to get up and down; otherwise, my desktop would become a launchpad.

The solution was pretty simple. I added two small step shelves on each side of the cabinets, creating on/off ramps on both sides so no one could get cornered. I used step shelves from ContempoCat, but you could make your own with any

basic shelf materials and some wall brackets or look for other small shelves at the home improvement store. I added sisal mats to the top surface, and it instantly became everyone's favorite hangout spot. Now I sit at my desk with cats looking down at me from above, and I can keep an eye on them as well. I love seeing them up there, and it's great having them nearby while I'm working. Plus it's nice that

they have their own special spot—not on my keyboard.

 Jackson

This kind of redefines cat TV—I mean, who's watching whom? The cats are watching you work, and you're watching them climb and nap above. That's pretty cool.

operation: catify kate's office! 129

Catification Essentials

Mats with a nonslip backing are a must-have in any Catified home. You'll see we use them in almost every project, especially on superhighways. They prevent cats from slipping while also

protecting surfaces from scratches. Particularly with senior cats, cats with mobility issues, or overweight cats, nonslip mats are a must because these cats have an especially hard time navigating slippery surfaces.

Place nonslip mats on the tops of tables, shelves, bookshelves, and cabinets—anywhere your cat might go. You can purchase thin doormats that have a rubber backing, or sisal rug remnants with a nonslip backing work well, too. Use scissors or a utility knife to cut the mats to just the right size and shape.

KATE'S PRO TIPS

Sisal rug remnants are one of my favorite Catification tools; I always keep some on hand. Sisal rug manufacturers bundle together the leftover scraps from making full-size rugs and sell them by the pound. I get mine on eBay. They usually come in strips ranging from 6 to 10 inches wide, which is just the right size for all kinds of Catification projects. You can get 5, 10, or 15 pounds at a time for $2 to $3 per pound.

Installing Cat Steps with Pelican Brackets

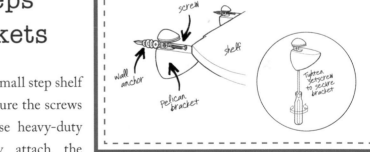

Pelican brackets are an attractive way to hang a small step shelf so it looks like it's floating. Be sure to either secure the screws into a wall stud or use heavy-duty wall anchors. Simply attach the brackets to the wall, slide the shelf into the brackets, and tighten the setscrew at the bottom of the bracket.

Pelican brackets come in a variety of shapes and finishes. You're sure to find something that matches your décor; check your local home improvement store for options.

SUBMITTED BY:
Wendy and David Hill;
Sunriver, Oregon

CATS:
Cooper and Izzy

the dresser drawer cat tower

RECYCLING AN OLD DRESSER TO CREATE THE ULTIMATE CAT HIDEOUT

Wendy and David were inspired by a creative repurposing project they saw using old dresser drawers to build a display shelf. Cats love to nap in drawers, so this is a perfect Catification project!

Wendy and David built their own very unique cat tower using repurposed dresser drawers for the climbing platforms and inexpensive boards for the frame. The finished dresser drawer cat tree stands about 70 inches tall and is very sturdy. Wendy notes, when planning your cat tree, be sure the cats can jump from one drawer to another easily. You might have to adjust the positioning and spacing of the drawers.

Materials and Budget

This project used six 2×2 boards and one used chest of five drawers. We spent $40 for the chest of drawers and $10 to $15 for the 2×2 boards. We searched craigslist, a junk shop, and used furniture stores to find just the right set of drawers for our project. We wanted them all to be the same size, slightly rectangular, not too big or too small. We took our time to find exactly what we wanted.

Wendy and David's Tips

It took two people to make the cat tower. We had decisions to make about the placement, but we just tried it out by holding the parts together before making it permanent. We liked the fact that the drawers were all wood, with a painted front and decorative knob.

The Result

Our cats love the tower! We added faux fur in two of the drawers for cat napping, which they appreciate. We kept moving it around until we found the spot they liked best, next to the refrigerator. It's a way up and down to the catwalk that we also installed. The tower provides another spot to watch us cook, it's great for roughhousing, and, finally, it's a great spot to take a nap.

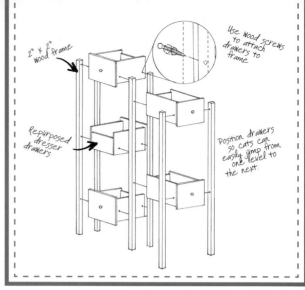

2" x 2" wood frame

Repurposed dresser drawers

Use wood screws to attach drawers to frame

Position drawers so cats can easily jump from one level to the next.

Seriously, what could make more sense than cats napping in drawers? This is brilliant! There are so many options for personalizing a project like this. You can choose any size or style of drawer to make one of these as funky or as refined as you like. The possibilities are endless! I love the repurposing aspect, too. It can really save you a lot of money, plus you're doing your part to keep old furniture from going to the landfill. Next time you're at the thrift store, take a look around and see if there are any other items that could be creatively repurposed for your cats.

SUBMITTED BY:
Dan and Jenne
Johnson; Wilmington,
North Carolina

CATS:
Bella, Mechat, Cali,
and Amber

cali's superhighway

This project features the extensive superhighway that Dan and Jenne built for their four cats Bella, Mechat, Amber, and, most important, Cali, their sweet senior cat. They wanted to boost Cali's confidence by giving her access to the vertical world, while giving all the cats plenty of ways to traverse the space without touching the ground. By providing lots of on/off ramps, this superhighway accommodates multiple cats beautifully.

We built the cat superhighway because 1) We saw it featured on Jackson's show and thought it was a great idea—our cats are so spoiled that they should have one; 2) with multiple cats, we are always concerned about giving them "safe" places to relax; and 3) Cali is getting older, and the other cats like to pressure her, so we wanted to give her a confidence boost because a confident cat is a happy cat!

Materials and Budget

We used floating shelves from IKEA and two amazing cat trees (best we've ever found) from CatVantage. The shelving was not expensive (about $200 for the twenty pieces we used). The cat trees were about $200 each. In total we spent about $600 on this project.

Jenne and Dan's Tips

The first step in completing this project was to conceptualize how we wanted to fit the superhighway into our living space. We used Jackson's formula for success and looked for multiple on/off ramp opportunities. That's when we discovered the CatVantage cat trees. They are sleek, easy to install, and flexible in their design—and our cats love them! The only challenge was figuring out how to hang the small shelves on two studs, because if they weren't attached to the studs, they wouldn't be secure enough to hold our sixteen-pounder. We ended up mounting them to a board that spanned the distance between the two studs.

The Result

Our cats all love the cat superhighway, and we think it is an amazing success! They don't all use it in the same way, though. Our natural climbers love to get up there and hang out, and our ground kitties will wait until the climbing kitties have gone up to pass through the room or to settle in a cozy chair. The superhighway just gives them so many more options and really adds dimension to their living space. We are interested in expanding it, and we even have materials and a plan to do so. Our next phase will be to punch through the wall between the living room and kitchen so the girls can get from their nap spot to their snack spot without ever having to touch the ground!

 *Jackson*

I love it! And they're right—a confident cat's a happy cat. This is a perfect example of someone building from that place of saying, what does my cat want and need? Dan and Jenne keep in mind that as Cali gets older, and as she's getting pressured by the other cats, her abilities to escape and to climb up to the vertical world are compromised. When a cat doesn't trust her body anymore as she gets older, she loses confidence as a prey animal. I would challenge Dan and Jenne to think about whether the cat tree alone is going to work for Cali in a year or two. They should start thinking about how to replace steps with ramps—basically how to modify traffic lanes to better accommodate a senior cat. Plan ahead, and be proactive. Aging is inevitable, so we might as well plan for it.

 Kate

What a beautiful solution that integrates so well with the décor! I love how the cats look like sculptures sitting on their shelves. And what a brilliant idea to attach the small shelves to a board so they can be mounted into the studs—excellent! It's always better to overbuild, making sure the shelves are more than strong enough to hold your cats, especially since running and jumping puts even more stress on the shelves. I can't wait to see phase two!

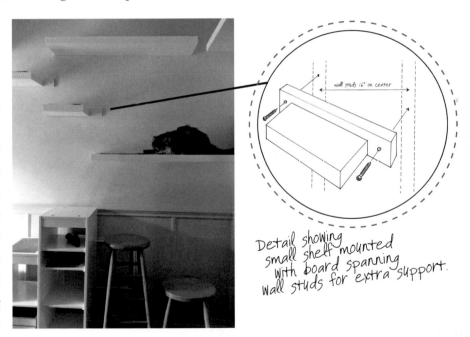

wall studs 16" on center

Detail showing small shelf mounted with board spanning wall studs for extra support.

No-Excuses Catification: Planter Cat Bed

This super-easy project makes use of any old planter pot—one you have sitting around the house or perhaps a thrift store find. Simply add a comfy cushion, and voilà! Instant cat bed that matches your décor. Or maybe your cat likes it just the way it is, sans cushion! No work at all.

Get up now and go to the garage or the basement and look for something to do this with! It doesn't have to be a planter—any container will do. How about a basket? Or a decorative storage bin? And you don't need a cushion; how about a blanket or a colorful towel instead? Just be imaginative and find something you like the look of. You have no excuses!

"I DON'T NEED NO STINKIN' CUSHION!"

SUBMITTED BY:
Ryan Davis;
Roseville, California

CATS:
Meesha and Sommers

kitty city

A CLIMBING STRUCTURE
WITH TWO CATWALKS

My mom and stepdad have two Bengal cats. They had been talking about building them some type of climbing structure that included catwalks but really didn't have any concrete ideas. They thought a good spot would be on the walls that met with a 45-degree angle cut out at the corner. I love to design and build things, and luckily they have a big workshop in the garage. I thought it would be cool to take advantage of the missing space (created by the 45-degree cutout) and also take advantage of the access to the shop tools.

My criteria for the design was climb, play, walk, and sleep, plus the design needed

to fit with the architecture and décor of the house. I achieved those goals by creating separate modules with different activities and incorporating the design of the modules to complement the existing furniture. By using that particular space, I could design the structure to be part of the 90-degree-angle corner where the two walls meet. Two of the modules have interior steps, and the top and bottom modules have cubbies. The modules also have shelves with a short barrier at the edges for sleeping. One of the catwalks has a 45-degree corner piece for sleeping. I also needed to be sure the cats wouldn't be able to climb from the modules to the existing shelving and the top of the TV. I cut two triangular blocks of wood and painted them the color of the wall. I put them on top of the two small square shelves. This prevented the cats from stepping from the modules to the top of the square shelves.

Inspiration came from the cats' love of climbing and the aesthetics that would need to fit in with the rest of the house's décor/furniture. I sketched up and played with a few foam-core model variations to be sure the structure would be functional and usable. The colors came from the cats themselves and the colors used in the rooms. One of the cats (Meesha) loves to climb up on top of the kitchen cabinets, so I knew she would love being up high on the catwalks. Every time I saw the cats play, I could tell they would love something like this. Bengals love to play, and they need a lot of stimulation. I wanted to design something that would give them some mental activity (navigating the structure) and also some exercise. The cats are energetic, playful, and part of the family household, so they need a space of their own. They both have their favorite sleeping spots, and as predicted, Meesha loves to hang out on the catwalks.

Materials and Budget

We built this project with simple materials from the home improvement store, plywood, 2×4s, and carpet. The total cost was around $325.

Ryan's Tips

First, I photographed the room to plan the structure and then I drew the concept design on the computer using the photographs. I then built a foam-core prototype of the three modular pieces to be sure the cats would be able to go up the steps inside. Using the foam-core prototype as a guide, I cut out all the wooden pieces and created the two catwalks, nailed and glued the pieces together, carpeted them, and mounted the entire structure on the wall. The biggest challenge was attaching the carpeting because it was difficult to get inside the modules.

FOAM-CORE MOCK-UP

kitty city (145)

WOOD FRAME BEFORE ATTACHING THE CARPET

 Jackson

First of all, I think this is great because it really is über stylish, but I love that at the corner we have multiple lanes of traffic. I love the top part where you have one lane leading down to another, and down to another. Catifying corners can be a little bit dicey, especially at that height when two cats are both headed toward the corner from different directions. This design really addresses that challenge by turning it into a superhighway at that corner. The way one lane dips down, it creates an alternate lane where cats can go if two are headed toward each other. That corner there is the brilliance of this design. Including the floor, there are seven lanes at the corner.

Of course, the next step would be to extend the superhighway out, but this goes to show that starting with a key piece like the corner, you really create a lot of opportunities to grow. The corner piece creates a hub to work from, allowing the design to be truly scalable and expandable.

 Kate

I think the end result looks like a piece of contemporary art, and it matches their décor very well. Clearly, this project took a bit of expertise, and Ryan is obviously an excellent woodworker, but no matter what your skill level is, take a cue from how he planned the design. I think it's really brilliant how he created a full-scale mock-up using foam core to test everything before final construction. This adds time to the process, but it's totally worth it because it lets you check out the design and really refine things before finishing.

escape from washing machine island

A Behind-the-Scenes Look at *My Cat from Hell*, Season 4, Episode 14

When Brenda and her cat, Kashmir, moved in with Dean and his cat, Darla, things did not go as smoothly as everyone had hoped. Brenda knew that Kashmir had a "mean streak," as evidenced by the scars on Brenda's hands, but when the couple moved in together, Kashmir's predator instincts spiked, and poor Darla immediately became her primary focus. On top of that, their home was well under 1,000 square feet. Darla was being stalked continuously and had no place to get away. The small apartment was filled with dead ends where Kashmir could corner Darla, cutting off her escape routes. The traffic flow in the space was a mess, allowing Kashmir to

KASHMIR

DARLA

dominate Darla in a fear-based relationship. The challenge here was to create an environment with free-flowing traffic where the two cats could live together peacefully—and make no mistake, it was a challenge.

KASHMIR CORNERING DARLA

escape from washing machine island 149

One of the first things I noticed when Darla walked in the room was that she immediately looked up. She was looking at shelves, at the tops of cabinets—her focus (and her territorial desires) rested entirely in the vertical world. I knew that if we listened to what she was telling us, we would uncover a confident tree dweller. My excitement about this discovery was dampened when I realized that Darla's primary "safe spot" was on top of the washing machine in the hallway. Safe perhaps, but completely removed from the social core of the home. If Darla remained exiled to Washing Machine Island, she would always be invisible. Although she would physically be in the vertical world, her confidence would be in the basement. We had to pull her out and expand her territorial confidence until she felt like she owned the whole place.

Scoping out the small space, I realized that this case called for classic urban planning. We had to build a cat superhighway with the objective of bringing Darla from her island to the living room, and from there to the couple's bedroom—an extremely significant social spot in every home because cats relish being near their people. While directing our attention to this

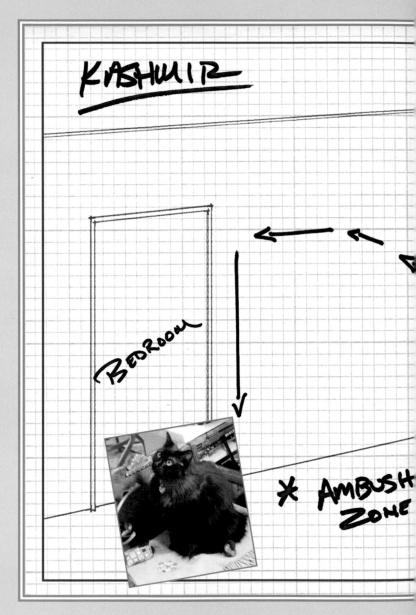

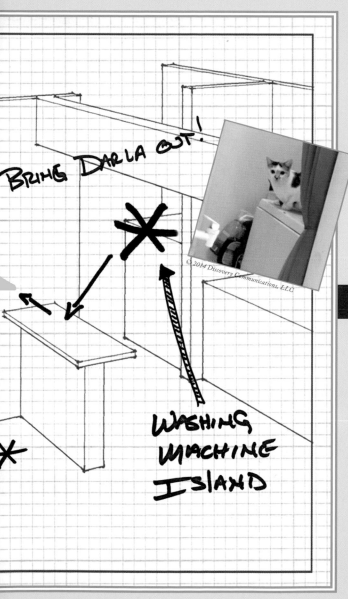

BRING DARLA OUT!

WASHING MACHINE ISLAND

task, we had to remember that the objective was integration. People think that when I call for a cat superhighway, I want the cats to live up there. Of course not! I wanted Darla to gain confidence in the higher spots where she already felt most at ease and then challenge her to make her way down until one day she finds herself face-to-face with Kashmir in the middle of the territory. In taking the long view, we had to bear in mind that we were dealing with a heavy traffic area that needed lane expansion and better traffic flow in order to avoid collisions. We had our work cut out for us, to say the least.

🐾 Kate

When I walked into Brenda and Dean's place, it was hard to take it all in because the space was so small and packed with furniture and all of their belongings—something that's pretty common when you combine two households. It looked like they had just started stuffing things in corners to make it all fit, and the result was a bit claustrophobic. They hadn't really given a lot of thought to the traffic flow, for either the humans or the cats. I knew my challenge would be to carve out an area that we could focus on in order to start giving some order to the chaos.

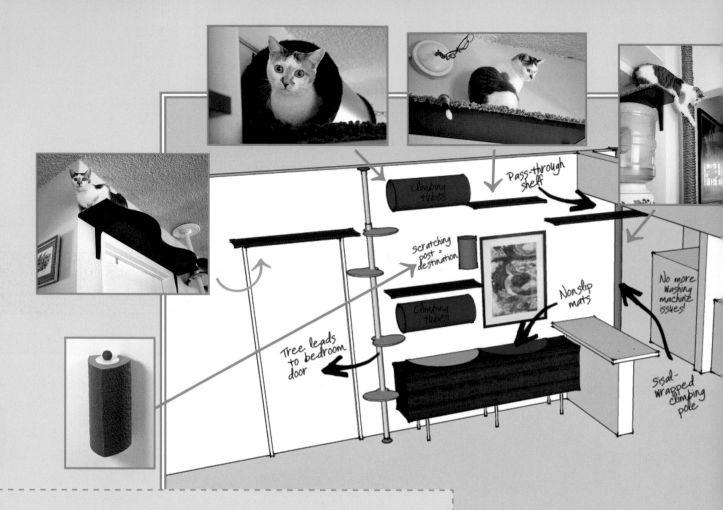

Climbing tubes

Pass-through shelf

Scratching post = destination

Climbing tubes

Nonslip mats

No more Washing machine issues!

Tree leads to bedroom door

Sisal-wrapped climbing pole

We started expanding Darla's territory by adding a floor-to-ceiling sisal-wrapped climbing pole in the kitchen, allowing her to shimmy up the pole to safety on a shelf that leads from the kitchen out to the dining area. There, she now has an entire superhighway with carpet-topped shelves and suspended climbing tubes leading to a cat tree that takes her directly to the door of Brenda and Dean's bedroom. Note the placement of the tubes in relation to the shelves. The tubes are cocoons, not caves. (Darla can choose to be in the

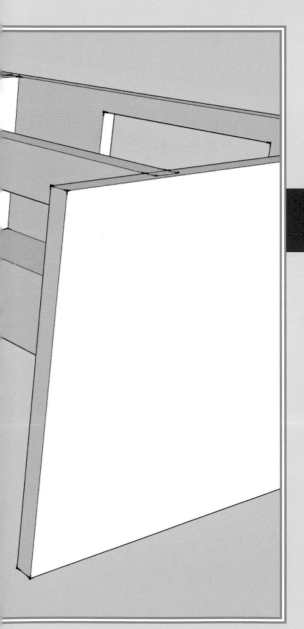

cocoon, but right next to it are the open shelves so she can choose to come out when she's ready.) We also cleared the clutter and incorporated the top of the credenza into the superhighway, adding nonslip mats to the top to invite Darla down into the mid-level range of the space.

Darla's superhighway includes the following elements:

- A **floor-to-ceiling sisal-wrapped climbing pole** in the kitchen gives Darla an on ramp for her superhighway.
- **Cat climbing shelves** extend the traffic lanes and are topped with carpet to prevent slipping.
- We cleared the top of the **credenza** below the shelves and added some nonslip mats. This is now a designated "cat only" surface and part of the highway.
- **Suspended climbing tubes** give Darla a place where she can be up high but hidden from view. No more evil glares from Kashmir below!
- Darla even has her own **wall-mounted cardboard scratcher** as a rest stop (and scent soaker) on her superhighway.
- The **tension pole cat tower** creates another on/off ramp for the superhighway.

CAT DADDY DICTIONARY

COCOON

What's the difference between a cocoon and a cave? A cave is a hermitage—a remote place where one goes to disappear, to hide, with no thought as to when one will emerge again. A cocoon is a safe place where one can rest that's located in a more socially accessible spot. A cave is a spot like the back of the closet or deep under the bed. A cocoon is a bed with a top on it put in the middle of the living space.

Also, true to its name, a cocoon encourages the act of metamorphosis; it affords its inhabitant the opportunity (and inspiration) to make a potentially courageous choice—to exit the hiding place and rejoin the outer world. When working to raise the confidence of a scared cat, we have to make them feel safe, while at the same time coaxing them to come out into the open where they will be vulnerable. The cocoon is an indispensable tool to help us balance comfort and challenge. Darla's cocoon tubes are both traffic lanes and destinations. One is enclosed, and the other is open. Giving her this side-by-side choice allows her to make the decision to come out into the wider world in her own time.

🐾 Jackson

Watching Darla navigate the finished superhighway was a moment of true exhilaration for me because this was an opportunity to hold a cat's hand and guide them into a brave place. To see Darla climb that pole and walk those shelves, hang out in the vertical world and eventually work her way down to the floor, was absolutely amazing. Beyond Darla's accomplishments, this project had numerous benefits. First, Kashmir was given more space to call her own. Because of that, her hair-trigger temper was diffused, and her aggression went down dramatically. We also achieved our goal of showing Brenda and Dean what was possible in their space. By Cat-ifying this one area, we gave them an example of what could be done throughout. When I walk away from a home like Brenda and Dean's, I want to be sure I haven't just put a Band-Aid on the situation, but that I have given them cat glasses and a mojo toolbox—and I think that's what we did here.

🐾 Kate

I love the end result of this project. It's colorful and fun, and we were even able to incorporate some of Brenda's original artwork into the climbing wall. Once we cleared the clutter and thought about how the traffic should flow from the kitchen into the liv-ing room, we came up with some unique features like the climb-

escape from washing machine island

ing pole and the pass-through shelf. I think elements like these add variety to the superhighway for the cats. Plus it's fun for the people to watch the cats use them. I hope Brenda and Dean will be inspired by what we did and will continue expanding the superhighway throughout the rest of the house.

Suspended Climbing Tubes

This project uses simple, inexpensive materials to create a kitty hideaway that hangs on the wall. You can choose to hang it up high or down low, depending on your cat's preference.

MATERIALS AND TOOLS

Cardboard concrete form tube (available at most home improvement stores), paint or decorative fabric for the outside of the tube, decorative edging material, carpet or sisal remnant for inside the tube, canvas or nylon straps for hanging, wall anchors with screws, finish washers, electric drill/driver, level, glue gun.

KATE'S PRO TIPS

Concrete form tubes are available in different diameters, ranging from 8 inches to 12 inches or larger. Choose a size that allows your cat to turn around easily. I like to use the 10-inch diameter.

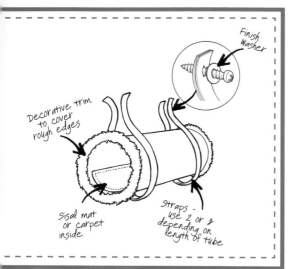

Finish washer

Decorative trim to cover rough edges

Sisal mat or carpet inside

straps - use 2 or 3 depending on length of tube

Instructions

Measure and cut the concrete tube to the desired length and paint the outside of the tube. You also could glue fabric to the outside. If the edges of the tube are rough from cutting, hot-glue decorative trim around each edge. Wrap two or three lengths of strap around the tube, and secure it to the wall using wall anchors as needed, putting the screws through both ends of the strap with a finish washer

Catification Essentials

If you have nosy cats or cats who are caving in lower cabinets or drawers where you don't want them, consider adding childproof locks to the doors and drawers. Another easy solution that's a little less cumbersome is to install heavy-duty magnet closures. These provide just enough pull to prevent your cat from opening the doors and drawers, but they still make it easy for you to open and close them.

SUBMITTED BY:
Sylvia and David Jonathan;
Costa Mesa, California

CATS:
Missy and Moose

the ultimate window perch

Here's a great little project from Sylvia and David Jonathan, who wanted to install a window perch so their cats could enjoy the view. Because they couldn't find a premade perch they liked, they made their own. They found a shelf piece and brackets at the home improvement store and added a simple cat bed to the top. The bed is held on with Velcro so it's easy to remove and clean, but it stays in place when the cats jump up on the perch.

Types of Shelf Brackets

It's easy to customize cat shelves and perches when you build your own. You can create just about anything you like to match your style and budget. When customizing cat shelves, consider the kind of shelf brackets you will use. Premade brackets are available in a wide variety of styles, from modern to traditional, from simple to ornate. Sylvia and David chose plain white shelf brackets with hidden hardware for a more contemporary look. Shelf brackets come in plastic, wood, and metal. Take a look at the organizing section of your home improvement store, or do a quick search online for shelf brackets to see the options. Here are a few examples, ranging from the most basic to elaborately decorative.

kitty box
hammock

The This project combines two of every cat's favorite things—a cardboard box and a comfy hammock. All you need are some simple tools and materials, and in no time, you'll have a fun new hangout spot your cat will be happy to call her own.

MATERIALS AND TOOLS

Cardboard box (at least 12 to 14 inches tall and 12 to 18 inches wide and deep), glue gun and glue sticks, metal straight-edge utility knife, scissors, fleece fabric.

This project was inspired by the SnoozePal, designed and made by Cat Above Company.

Instructions

Cut openings in all four sides of your box, leaving 3 inches around all four edges of each side of the box. Seal the box closed on top and bottom using hot glue.

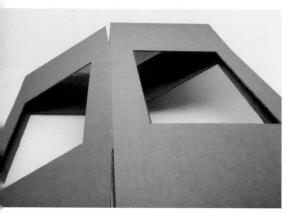 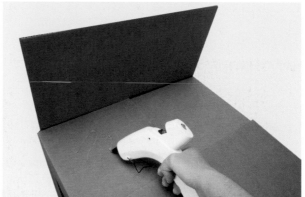

With the tip of your scissors, punch holes midway between the top and bottom in the middle of each edge piece.

Cut the fleece to extend beyond your box 4 inches on all four sides. For example, if your box measures 18 inches by 18 inches, cut your fabric 26 inches by 26 inches (18 + 4 + 4 = 26). Cut 4-inch slits in each corner of the fleece.

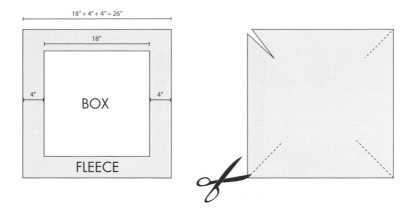

18" + 4" + 4" = 26"

18"

4"

BOX

4"

FLEECE

Insert the points of fleece through the holes in the edges, and tie in a knot.

G et creative! Try raising or lowering the height of the hammock, experiment with different box sizes, and place a soft blanket or piece of carpet in the bottom to create a multilevel lounger!

SAFETY PRECAUTIONS

When repurposing a used cardboard box for your cat, be sure to remove any possible choking hazards.

Packing Tape

Staples

Labels

Plastic Envelopes

Tear Strips

SUBMITTED BY:
Lucio Castro;
Brooklyn, New York

CATS:
Violet, Cleo, and America

scratch this!

TABLE LEG SCRATCHER

I wanted to build a scratcher for my cats, but I had noticed two things: 1) they hated an unstable scratcher, and 2) the scratcher needed to be tall enough that they could also stretch while scratching. And the more it looked like a real tree, the better. Space is tight, since I live in New York (and I don't really like the look of "typical cat furniture" or how much space it takes up), so I decided to wrap one of the wooden legs of my table with sisal rope. My cats immediately loved it, and it was super cheap, looked good, and took no extra space.

Materials and Budget

Sisal rope, a few nails, and a hammer. Less than $10.

Lucio's Tips

I have no DIY experience at all, so it was as easy and as fast as it can be. I just wrapped the sisal rope around a wooden table leg and hammered a few nails into the back to keep it in place.

The Result

They all loved it right away. It was and still is amazing.

Let me tell you how much I love this. First, it costs less than $10, so this should be within everyone's budget. Second, Lucio had no DIY experience, so anyone can do this! And third, he really thought about it from the cat's point of view. Bravo!

Follow Lucio's lead, and look at your Catification project from the same perspective he did. He noticed that his cats like to stretch while scratching, but they don't like an unstable scratcher. He doesn't like regular cat furniture, so he looked around for something in his home he could use instead, and he came up with something the cats love. Bingo.

It couldn't be any more

of a success for the cats because he came at it from an organic perspective. This is what I want everyone to do: Come at your Catification project from your cat's viewpoint first. Think about what your cat wants and then make it work in your world, not the other way around.

 Kate

The simplicity of this project makes me giddy! I think it's absolutely brilliant, and it makes me want to run around my house wrapping everything in sisal rope. Think about the possibilities!

Lucio didn't use hot glue to keep the rope in place, like you'll see in some other examples we show you, but in this case, that was probably a good choice because he may want to replace the rope when it is worn out, and that will be a lot easier to do if it's not glued. He used nails to secure the rope to the wooden table leg. You could also use screws, but try to avoid using staples because they could pull out and become a choking hazard for cats.

When you think about Catifying your house, the first thing you have to consider is *What is my cat asking for?* And then everything else falls into place.

REESE

...

*Guard Cat
Extraordinaire*

a guard cat goes to her "happy place"

A Behind-the-Scenes Look at *My Cat from Hell*, Season 5, Episode 11

REESE GUARDING DOOR

REESE GUARDING FROM COUNTER

If you wanted to get in the door at Beth and George's home in San Diego, you had to get past their cat Reese, the anti-Mojito Cat. Instead of greeting you at the door with a tray of hors d'oeuvres, she told you, in no uncertain terms, that you were trespassing. Many, if not most, visitors to Beth and George's house wound up intimidated or, in a few instances, bloody. This tortie was all about protecting her home, and she made sure to let visitors know who was in charge. Reese's territorial sense of ownership of Beth and George's home was clearly out of balance.

Reese had set up a guard post in the front window that faces the door so she could clearly see all the comings and goings. She paced back and forth there, looking like a caged animal. As with all caged animals, when the door opens, they uncoil like a snake. Furthermore, she saved her most intimidating aggression for Beth and George if either of them tried to remove her from her guard post.

In addition, Beth and George were both suffering from a bad case of crazy cat lady phobia. Specifically, whenever we tried to begin the discussion about how they could put Catification to work in their home, Beth seemed to have visions of pink shag carpet everywhere. She was absolutely panicked that Kate was going to turn her house into the crazy cat lady house.

REESE GUARDING FROM WINDOW

a guard cat goes to her "happy place"

I was at a loss because the geographic position of both the window and the door was incredibly frustrating. There was no place to redirect Reese. Everything was a dead end. The kitchen was like a black hole; there was no way to lead her out of the space and away from her attack spot at the door. There was so little to work with, yet I knew that making the environment more fluid was the key to getting Reese 1) away from guarding that area, and 2) more confident in the first place so she didn't feel the need to guard the area. That all sounds simple, but that's why I called Kate, because even I was beginning to think the situation was impossible. I was at a complete loss with this one.

🐾 Kate

Once I saw the real challenges of the architecture, I knew a superhighway was not a possible solution, so we de-

cided to focus on the window area. I had to come up with something that Reese would find more desirable than guarding. She had absolutely nothing to do in the window except pace and focus on whoever came to the front door, at which point she would spring into action and attack. She was so focused on the "intruders" that she had no sense of curiosity about other things in her environment. Birds and bugs outside the window became just an annoyance instead of something to watch and engage with. I also noticed that Beth and George didn't have a lot of cat-specific things in their home, just a single cat tree in the living room. Reese really needed some areas she could mark and call her own, but we had to do it in a way that would make Beth and George happy, alleviating their fears.

We had to prevent Reese from hunkering down in the window and guarding the front door; that was key. Instead, we had to give her the sense of doing a job that's not guarding. We had to add fluid motion to the space, give her opportunities for play, and keep her occupied in the space.

Our goal was to give Reese ownership of the window area, adding items she could scent mark and things to entertain her. But it wasn't just a matter of distracting her; it was about changing this place, in her mind, from her first line of defense to a play area, a great, fun spot. And that was a tall order.

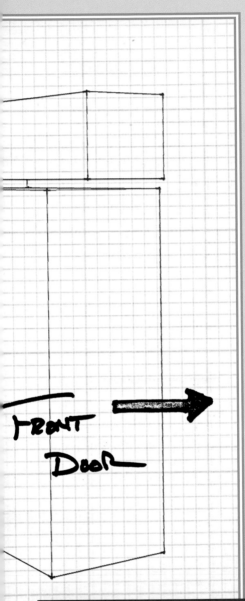

FRONT DOOR →

WINDOW BEFORE WITH NOTHING IN IT FOR REESE TO OWN, NOTHING TO DISTRACT HER. (PHOTO ON RIGHT SHOWS RELATIONSHIP OF WINDOW TO FRONT DOOR.)

We filled the window and surrounding area with an assortment of features to change it up and make it a place Reese could call her own.

- **Sisal ramp** leads from the window to the top of the refrigerator, giving Reese an alternate route and moving her through the space. The sisal also allows her to scratch and leave her scent, helping her own the space.

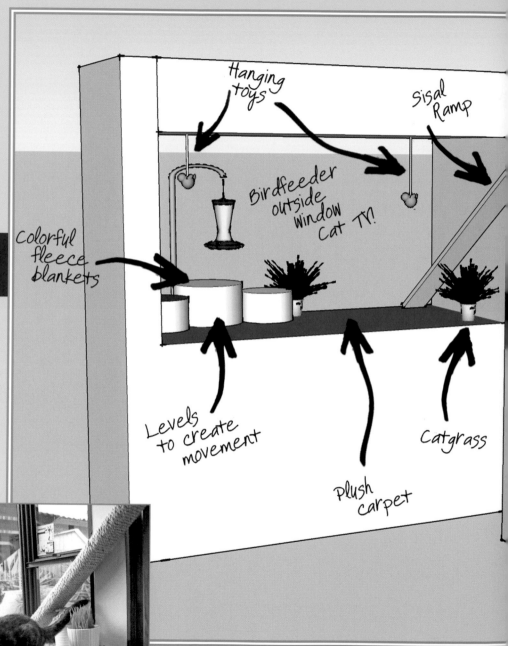

Hanging toys

Sisal Ramp

Colorful fleece blankets

Birdfeeder outside Window Cat TV!

Levels to create movement

Plush carpet

Catgrass

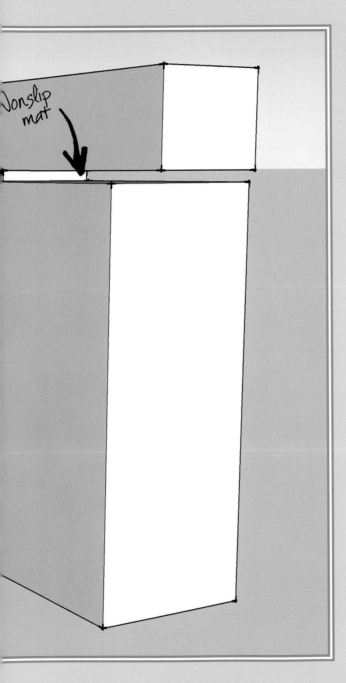

- **Nonslip mat** on the top of the fridge prevents slipping and gives her a soft spot to rest.
- Thick **carpet** on the windowsill gives her another place to leave her scent and prevents slipping.
- Live **cat grass** plants provide Reese with something to munch on as a distraction.
- **Levels** created with upturned storage bins give her a little place to climb and keep the flow of movement through the window area. We also added soft **fleece blankets** to the tops of the levels as another scent soaker and as a decorative feature.
- **Hanging bird toys** distract and entertain.
- **Birdfeeder** directly outside window makes cat TV—more entertainment and distraction.

CAT DADDY DICTIONARY
CAT TV

When we think of sitting in front of the television, we instantly go to a place where we kick up our feet, find something to hold our attention, forget the troubles of the day . . . and zone out. Yes, just like humans can be hypnotized by something on television, cats can be hypnotized by looking out a window; at an aquarium; or at a bird, bug, or fish. The hypnosis in question, though, is anything but zoning out; it's *tuning in*.

By literally presenting a window onto potential prey, the Raw Cat's engine is ignited. A big component of hunting is *watching*. Remember, that moment of pounce is only that; the rest is sizing up, playing cat chess in their minds, thinking of every possible move, and assessing the patterns of movement and the speed of those movements. Don't for a moment think, when you watch your cat stare out a window—something they do on a daily basis more than even sleep—that they are zoning out. In fact, it is just the opposite. Cat TV is passive engagement.

When you look at a room and think about Catifying, your first stop should be the windows. Ask yourself, if you were your cat, what is out every window that could ignite your mojo? Then, add things outside the window like birdfeeders or plants and flowers that will attract birds and

insects. At the same time, be sure to make the window itself a proper destination with a ledge or a bed that allows your cat to sit comfortably and watch the world.

Boredom is the mother of chaos in homes with cats, and cat TV is the ultimate solution for that boredom. It can also diffuse fights between multiple cats and combat separation anxiety if your cat has behavior issues when being left alone. It provides cats with an outlet for the only job they have—hunt, catch, kill, eat—so by providing that outlet for these activities, you're helping prevent a whole host of problems.

No-Excuses Catification: Catnip and Cat Grass

Adding containers of fresh cat grass or catnip around the house is a cheap and easy way to give your cat a tasty snack that aids her digestion, provides her with the greens cats get in the wild, and gives her something else she can own. You've probably got an empty container hanging around the house, and it's really easy to grow your own plants and grass from seed, which costs next to nothing. You don't even have to have a green thumb! Or you can purchase pregrown plants from a nursery or pet supply store. You have absolutely no excuse!

BEHIND THE SCENES (WHAT YOU DIDN'T SEE ON THE SHOW)

We also added a cat tree in the dining area. This tree has carpet-covered platforms—another place for Reese to leave her scent so she feels like she owns

the tree. Reese likes to be on the kitchen counter, so this gives her an alternate way to access the counter; plus, the tree has a direct line of sight to the front door, but it's far enough away, Reese can sit on her tree and calmly observe visitors entering through the front door, rather than ambushing them with an attack. We made sure to add a sisal scratching post at the top of the tree for an extra scent-marking opportunity.

DINING AREA AFTER

a guard cat goes to her "happy place" 181

DINING AREA BEFORE

At the end of the day, this project was about giving Reese a "jackpot" focused activity that was also acceptable to the humans she lives with. That was the tough part. She considered guarding a very high-value activity, and connected to guarding was pacing, so by funneling her physically and mentally toward the middle of the window area, we eliminated the pacing. This is a great example of dead ends being the mother of invention; we had to focus her in the space.

We really had to get into Reese's head and visualize how she was seeing things—the empty window area, people entering through the door and threatening her territory, her lack of things to own. Once we understood her perspective, we were able to Catify her space and redirect her energy.

🐾 *Kate*

The end result seems to be a success. Reese took to her new window area almost immediately and actually seemed calmer in her new hangout spot. She loved the cat grass and catnip plants, and she even stood right up and engaged with the hanging bird toys. (That was exciting!) The overall look of the window area brings the outside garden in, making the design flow visually.

No-Excuses Catification: Birdfeeder Cat TV

This one is so easy! Simply add a birdfeeder outside any window in your home to make instant cat TV. Hang one from a tree or off the edge of a roof, or use a plant stand that sticks in the ground. Be sure to give Kitty access to the window and make her a comfy place to sit and watch the show. Also be sure the birdfeeder caters to the bird population native to your area. San Diego is highly populated with hummingbirds, which is why we chose this feeder for Reese. Get up and go do this right now!

Ramp It Up!
How to Make a Simple Sisal Ramp

This project uses basic materials available from any home improvement store to create a simple ramp that can be used in all kinds of situations. Use it as training wheels to help your cat become familiar with climbing from one surface to another, and remove it when she gets the hang of it. You also can keep moving the ramp from one place to another to keep things interesting for your cat. The sisal provides a great scratching surface and a place to mark.

a guard cat goes to her "happy place" 183

TRAINING WHEELS

The sisal ramp leading from the window to the top of the fridge is an example of training wheels. These are devices that can be used temporarily to test out different Catification elements or to challenge a cat to try something new, without committing to a permanent change. The sisal ramp is easily removable, so if Reese isn't using it, or if Beth and George find that Reese isn't behaving when she's on the top of the fridge, they can remove the ramp and try it someplace else.

Other ways to use training wheels would be to add ramps or temporary steps to help your cat get up onto a new shelf; then, when she's comfortable jumping up by herself, you can remove the training wheels.

Training wheels give you an easy way to change the landscape.

This tool illustrates the connection between Catification and behavior. By switching up the environment, you're constantly creating challenges for the Raw Cat. In the wild, a branch falls where it wasn't yesterday, creating new possibilities on the vast cat chessboard. Add a new element, like a sisal ramp, and before your cat gets bored of it, move it to a new location. Training wheels, in essence, exercise that crucial part of the Raw Cat mind.

MATERIALS AND TOOLS

2×4 or any other size board, any size sisal or manila rope (we used ⅜ inch), hot-glue gun and glue sticks, electric drill, scissors or utility knife.

KATE'S PRO TIPS

- -

Check the lumber-scrap bin at the home improvement store for small pieces of wood. Sometimes they have just what you need, and it's discounted!

This one is really easy! Drill a hole in the end of the board, slightly larger than the thickness of your rope. I used a ½-inch drill bit with ⅜-inch sisal rope, and it fit perfectly. Use some hot glue to secure one end of the rope in the hole, and start wrapping the rope around the board. Glue the rope as you continue wrapping. When you get to the other end of the board, drill another hole and insert the end of the rope with some more hot glue.

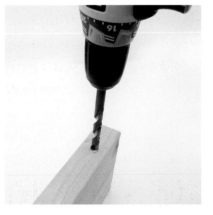

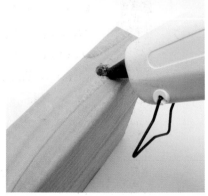

When cutting sisal rope, wrap a piece of tape around the rope and cut through the tape with scissors or a utility knife. This helps keep the ends of the rope from fraying.

Easy No-Sew Fleece Blanket

Soft blankets make for perfect scent soakers, and they have the added benefit of covering your furniture so you can simply toss them in the washing machine. It's good to have a bunch of these around so you can always have a clean one out and a couple in the laundry.

MATERIALS AND TOOLS

Fleece fabric, scissors.

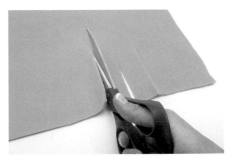

Fleece is an excellent material to use for easy, no-sew projects because it does not fray on the edges. Plus, it goes right in the washer and dryer with no fuss. Fleece is available at most craft or fabric stores and comes in a huge variety of colors and patterns.

An easy way to make a fun fleece blanket is to cut two pieces of fleece the same size, adding 4 inches extra on each side. For example, if you want your finished blanket to be 16 inches by 16 inches, cut the fleece 24 inches by 24 inches (16 + 4 + 4 = 24). Next, cut strips approximately 1 inch wide and 4 inches long around the edges, as shown in the diagram. Discard the corner pieces, and tie each set of strips together. Use two different colors or patterns of fleece for a reversible blanket.

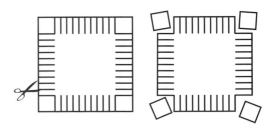

For Reese, I made round blankets to fit on the tops of her climbing levels. I traced a circle around each bin, making it 4 inches larger on all sides, cut the strips, and tied them together. They fit perfectly.

Hanging Cat Toys

Reese's window had a glass ceiling, so I decided to use suction cups to hang some toys in the middle of the area. I couldn't find any at the store that were just what I wanted, so I made my own. Here's how I did it.

MATERIALS AND TOOLS

Large suction cups, store-bought cat toys, shock cord (this is a stretchy cord, like bungee cord that comes in a variety of thicknesses—I used ⅛ inch), scissors, needle, and thread.

This is super simple! First I removed the hooks from the suction cups—you won't need those—and then I attached one end of the shock cord to the suction cup by wrapping it around the top piece and tying it in a knot. Next, I cut the shock cord to the length needed, leaving about an inch extra. I tied a small knot at the end of the cord and used the needle and thread to sew the cord to the toy, sewing through the knot for a good, firm hold. That's it!

You can customize this project with any toy from the store or with a toy you make yourself. The bird toys I used make a chirping noise when Kitty bats at them, adding an extra-fun feature.

KATE'S PRO TIPS

When cutting shock cord, melt the end just a little with a lighter or match. This will keep it from fraying.

One of the first things Reese noticed in her new window were the dangling bird toys. She jumped up immediately to bat at them, and she loved the bird noises they made.

a guard cat goes to her "happy place" 189

SUBMITTED BY:

Chris and Michelle Julius; Orlando, Florida

CATS:

Mittens and Bootsie

shelve it!

CHRIS AND MICHELLE JULIUS CREATE THE PERFECT CAT CLIMBER FOR THEIR CATS

Chris and Michelle built this awesome climbing wall for their cats, Mittens and Bootsie, using Lack shelves from IKEA. Take a look at the climber on the left. This is a brilliant Catification hack that's really easy to do!

CAT DADDY DICTIONARY

 CATIFICATION HACK

Catification hacks are a true test of your creativity. It's when you buy an off-the-shelf product, one that was never meant to be used by a cat, and put on your mojo glasses and turn it into something unique and cool for your cats.

the kitty climber

HOW TO CREATE A SIMPLE WALL-MOUNTED CAT CLIMBER

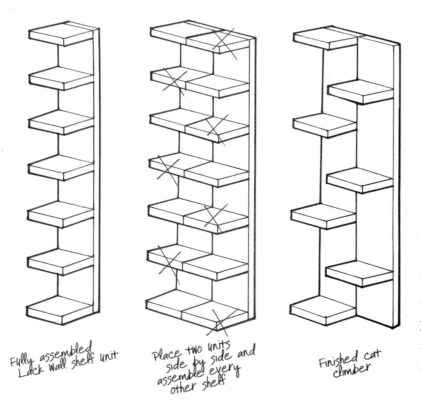

Fully assembled Lack Wall shelf unit

Place two units side by side and assembled every other shelf

Finished cat climber

Here's an easy way to create a simple wall-mounted cat climber that has a nice, modern look. This was created with two Lack wall shelf units from IKEA (such a great place for products to use for Catification hacks!). When you assemble the Lack shelves, use only every other shelf, leaving off the alternating shelves. Then position the two units on the wall as shown to create cat stairs. It just so happens that when you hang them this way, the shelves are perfectly spaced for cats to climb. Simple!

a wall scratcher that will make your cat purr with delight

Carpet tiles are great for a lot of Catification projects, like this easy wall scratcher. Simply cut the tiles to fit the area you want to cover, and use a nontoxic adhesive to attach them to the wall. Create decorative patterns and textures that match your décor while giving your cat an awesome vertical scratching surface.

KATE'S PRO TIPS

My favorite source for carpet tiles is FLOR. All kinds of colors and patterns are available, and you can order as many or as few tiles as you need for your project. I especially like the House Pet line of tiles because they are extremely durable, they come in a variety of beautiful colors, and they are made with cut fibers instead of looped. A cat's claws can get caught on looped carpet, but with the cut carpet, they can easily rake their claws through the fibers.

a wall scratcher that will make your cat purr with delight

SUBMITTED BY:
Eliane Gama and
Marccello Pistilli;
São Paulo, Brazil

CATS:
Torresmo, Sardinha,
Pudim, Sissa, Suzy,
and Sulu

ARCHITECT:
Monica Migliori Semeraro

tunnel vision

CREATING THE PERFECT CAT TUNNEL

Eliane and Marccello installed this awesome L-shape cat tunnel to give their six cats a place of their own. Take a closer look at the ends of the tunnel—there are doors on each end that can be closed off. What a great idea if you need to reach your cats for a vet visit or in case of an emergency. Simply close off the tunnel so they can't hide. Excellent idea!

a game of pip and red

HOW CATIFICATION HELPED RESTORE PEACE IN ONE FAMILY'S HOME

A Behind-the-Scenes Look at *My Cat from Hell,* Season 4, Episode 6

On one of his trips to San Francisco, Jackson was called in to help with two cats, Pip and Red. This was a unique situation because Pip has a condition known as cerebellar hypoplasia, which affects his coordination, making it hard for Pip to walk across the floor and completely impossible for him to climb anything, so he was 100 percent floor-bound. Despite his disability, Pip was instigating fights with Red, the other cat in the house, to the point that Red would escape outside through a skylight to get away from Pip. Red was then relegated to wandering the Oakland streets, susceptible to all of the inherent dangers cats face outside. This was a complicated case with many facets, and Catification played a major role in solving the problems between these two cats.

Cerebellar hypoplasia, also referred to as CH, is a neurological condition affecting both cats and dogs. It occurs when the cerebellum, the part of the brain that controls fine motor skills and coordination, is underdeveloped at birth. Cats with CH have difficulty walking; they move with jerky motions and often fall down. CH does not improve or worsen with age, and animals with the condition can live a normal life span.

 Jackson

This case was immediately intriguing to me because here you have Pip, a CH cat who is actually considered a bully, which is so unexpected because he can barely stand up; yet he was causing Red to flee in terror. Red was so desperate to get out of Pip's way that he popped out through the skylight of the house. It struck me right away that we've obviously got a Tree Dweller in Red here, and we've got a default Bush Dweller in Pip, who can't even climb the stairs. He is absolutely relegated to the floor. If this were a normal situation with two able-bodied cats, I'd be introducing them through opposite sides of the door—using food to form a positive association, and then graduating to other social exercises like tandem play—but I couldn't. I couldn't do all the normal things with a CH cat in the mix. Not only is Pip aggressive, but he's so unpredictable. And there's the rub. Red is instantly terrified of Pip, even before he comes at Red, because all Red sees is Frankenstein thrashing around. I had to help this Tree Dweller observe the physical patterns and behaviors of this crazy, floor-bound creature. Red was probably thinking to himself, *What is this thing coming at me? He doesn't look like a cat. He doesn't move like a cat. What is he?* My job was to create a setup where Red could observe Pip from a comfortable distance.

PIP'S PLAY MAT

Jackson

For Pip, my main challenge was to increase his confidence. I had a hunch that part of what Pip was experiencing was frustration. I think that he was frustrated with his inability to get what he wanted to get and to go where he wanted to go. One of the things we know about cerebellar hypoplasia is that as a cat's stress level increases, so do the tremors. Pip was making his own situation worse. So in

Catifying Pip's world, it came down to making the floor a source of confidence and attainable goals.

The answer became Pip's play mat. We kind of stumbled on this solution when we started by adding a variety of different textures to the floor to see which ones Pip would gravitate to. We experimented by putting a whole bunch of different types of mats, rugs, et cetera on the floor to see which would be the most appealing. One of the rugs happened to have big loops, and we started inserting toys into the loops, and surprisingly, Pip took to it immediately. The loops held the toys in place so they weren't moving around and getting away from him and frustrating him. The activity of playing with the now-stationary toys became something he could do for hours. It focused him in a way nobody had ever seen before. This is a great example of Catification being therapeutic. The solution was completely unexpected, but it gave us exactly the results we were looking for.

RED'S SUPERHIGHWAY

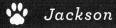

I wanted to create a really pleasing vertical world for Red. I decided to start building Red's superhighway at the stairs. Because Pip couldn't go up and down the stairs, but Red could, it made sense to start Red off from this area because he was

already using the stairs to get away from Pip. So we added a corner cat shelf at the landing of the stairs and then built out the superhighway from there. We took Red from the corner shelf over to the dining room table, and then to the wall. With a series of shelves and wall-mounted cat stairs, we extended Red's super-highway all the way around the room, ending at the door with a lookout perch where Red could sit instead of dashing out the door to get away from Pip.

I wanted Red to be so entranced by his new superhighway that he wouldn't feel the need to escape, and he'd have a safe vantage point from which to observe Pip. I also wanted to give him options for coming closer and closer to the floor, so he could start checking out Pip from a closer distance. We wanted to keep inching him down until finally that day would come when he would be comfort-able on the floor with Pip. To do this, we made sure the superhighway had lanes at every level. We paved the road for him and gave him the option to, over time, come down.

CAT DADDY DICTIONARY

 **SCALABILITY** 🐾

When Catifying, you need to be sure to cover the bases environmentally to accommodate your cat's changing needs; in other words, you need to think about scalability. Cats will change—from day to day and over time—to reflect their experience, long-term growth, and maturation. With every lesson learned comes wisdom, and from wisdom comes the desire to push boundaries and spread one's wings; your Catification design should accommodate that desire.

No-Excuses Catification: Terrarium Cat TV

In addition to using windows for cat TV, consider making a terrarium to keep your cat entertained, like we did for Red. His terrarium contained butterflies and other bugs, along with the plants, adding movement and interest. Be

sure to use a container that is securely sealed so your cat can't open it and get at the critters inside. Also, pick a sturdy container that isn't easily knocked over, and place it in a safe location away from the edge of the table.

🐾 *Jackson*

The Pip and Red case was an unbelievable success—this is one where I will look back and say, "Wow! This is what you can do when you think outside the box." We were able to make a change that, to be completely honest, I didn't think was possible, and the Catification was a critical piece of the puzzle. Once Red had a place up high where he could sit back, relax, and assess the situation, it changed everything for these two cats. The other part of the equation was that with Pip's play rug, we discovered how Catification can be functional and therapeutic.

© 2014 Discovery Communications, LLC

SUBMITTED BY:
Gerda and Jose Lobo;
Tempe, Arizona

CATS:
Liath, Arleigh, Arbolina,
Stanley, Irmo, Dido, Zaria,
Simone, Dark Matter,
Lucy, and Yani

gerda and jose lobo's living room racetrack

When we moved into our new house, we wanted to make the environment as friendly as possible for our multiple cats. Most of our cats tend to gather around us wherever we are; they do not really spread out much, which usually means there are occasional spats and hisses as they negotiate for space

around us. The house we moved into had a built-in shelf all the way around the living room and dining room about twelve inches from the ceiling, previously used for display. We decided to install a cat superhighway using the existing "ceiling shelf" as a starting point.

We wanted to keep the décor in the living room minimalist

and decided not to hang any art or have bookshelves or other display furniture against the walls. We figured the cats would be our kinetic art installation.

We were not exactly sure how to build this, but luckily Kate is a good friend and she offered to come over and help. Kate figured out the traffic patterns, planned the destination spots, added on/off ramps, and created extra traffic lanes so the cats wouldn't run into one another as they navigated their new superhighway.

I'm glad Gerda and Jose called me in to help with their Catification—this was a fun project! We were trying to be budget-conscious so we reused shelves from their old house and only added a few new pieces. We wanted to be sure there were plenty of on/off ramps for the cats because this is definitely a high-traffic house with eleven cats. Not all of them are Tree Dwellers, though, so by adding the superhighway, it allows some of the cats to go up, leaving more space on the ground for the bush and beach dwellers. Here are some of the elements we added to the superhighway:

- The **existing shelves** running all the way around the room were the perfect start for this cat superhighway.
- We added **cat shelves** on two walls so the cats could climb up to the racetrack.
- The **existing furniture** is used as part of the highway to help cats reach the climbing shelves.
- Two **crosspieces** create extra lanes to keep the traffic flowing smoothly.
- A **floor-to-ceiling sisal-wrapped climbing pole** provides an alternate way for cats to climb up to the shelves—plus it serves as a scratcher and scent soaker.
- The sisal pole is offset from the wall, creating a **pass-through** that allows the cats to pass between the pole and the wall on the climbing shelves.
- A **wraparound shelf** extends beyond the top shelf, allowing for easy access; plus, it wraps through into the kitchen area, where there is another on/off ramp and access to more built-in display shelving.

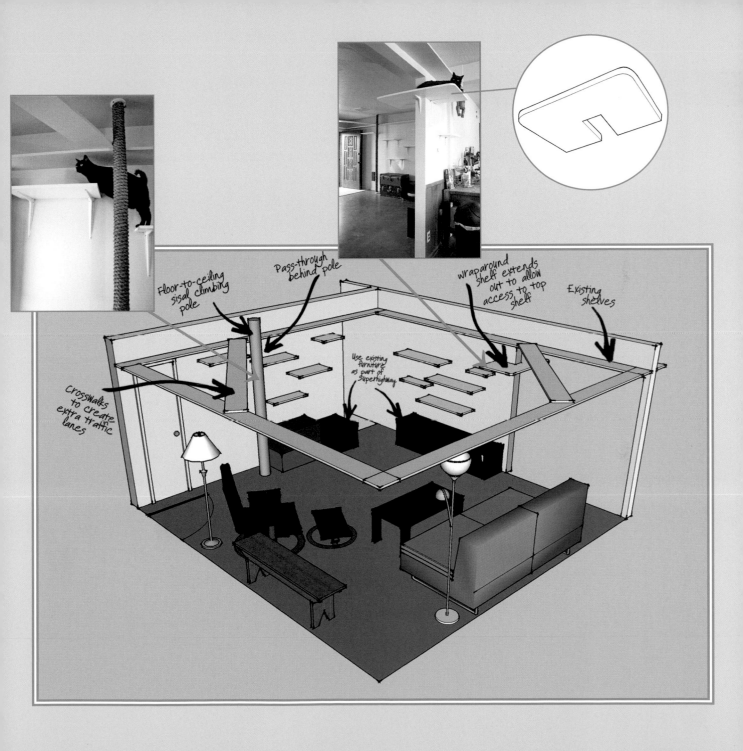

Floor-to-ceiling sisal climbing pole

Pass-through behind pole

wraparound shelf extends out to allow access to top shelf

Existing shelves

Use existing furniture as part of superhighway

Crosswalks to create extra traffic lanes

My favorite part is the U-shape shelf that wraps around the wall into the kitchen. I've always wanted to make one of these, but they only work in openings like this where there's no door. I love watching the cats as they walk around the shelf and pop out in the other room. It's kind of like a secret passageway, and it was really easy to make.

Gerda and Jose's Tips

It helped to build the project in stages. That way we could observe very carefully how much space the cats needed between shelves, and how far the shelves had to stick out so they would use them to move around and as perches.

The Result

The cats quickly learned how to use their new space. Some of our more attention-seeking felines jump up on the shelves facing the front door when they hear us come home, so we can see them (or see our wall art installation) the second we open the door. Our two very shy and nervous cats, Arbolina and Arleigh, now spend a lot of time with us and the other cats in the room, as they can quickly jump from floor to shelf to ceiling shelf and find the highest, safest spot from where they can look down on everybody. Our doofus cat, Liath, loves to run laps around the ceiling shelf, which goes around the entire room. When he sees me, he sprints up to the top shelf and starts running around and around, and he keeps doing that as long as I run along with him, underneath him. Sometimes we find one cat chasing another playfully along the ceiling "track," but it is all in good fun, because as soon as someone gets too worked up, they can just jump down one of the exit ramps.

climb this! creating the perfect floor-to-ceiling climbing pole

MATERIALS AND TOOLS

- Stolmen post (available from IKEA stores or ikea.com)
- Sisal or manila rope (we used ¾-inch-thick manila rope available from any home improvement store)
- Glue gun and glue sticks
- Small screws
- Electric drill/driver
- Pencil
- Level
- Scissors or utility knife

KATE'S PRO TIPS

- -

The length of rope you need depends on the thickness of rope you're using and the height of your finished climbing pole. Sisal and manila rope come in thicknesses ranging from ¼ inch to 1 inch. The ¼ inch looks nice, but think of how much wrapping you'll have to do if you use the smaller size!

As an example, for this project, I used ¾-inch-thick manila rope, and the finished pole was about 9 feet tall. I used about 100 to 125 feet of rope for this particular project. The ¾-inch rope is available in 150-foot spools at the home improvement store, or you can order it online from Amazon or most home building supply sites. That way, you'll have a little left over for another project. Using the thicker rope makes the finished climbing pole much wider, as well, giving your cat a nice solid surface to grab on to.

This is a pretty simple project, but there are some tricks to help it go smoothly for you. The Stolmen system from IKEA is a pretty brilliant thing. It uses telescoping posts that fit snugly between the floor and ceiling as the frame for hanging various shelves and drawers to create a modular storage system. The system offers a lot of creative possibilities using the components available at IKEA; however, you can also use just the post to make some awesome Catification hacks, including this project. What's great about it is that you can customize the climbing pole to the height of your ceiling because the Stolmen post adjusts from 82⅝ inches to 129⅞ inches.

Basically, you are going to fit the Stolmen post to the area where you want to install the climbing pole. Then you take it down, make a few adjustments to it to secure it, and wrap the whole thing in rope to create an awesome climbing and scratching surface. Once the post is wrapped, you simply put it in place, tighten the hardware, secure it to the ceiling (this is optional), and let your cats go to town. This is a great addition to any cat superhighway, but keep in mind that because of the direction of a cat's claws, she can easily climb up a pole like this but she won't be able to climb back down. This means the pole should only be considered an on ramp, not an off ramp, but it does make for a nice territory marker, too.

Step 1: Assembling the post. Assemble the Stolmen post pieces as outlined in the instructions that came with it. Basically, attach the large nut to the bolt that comes with the post, and insert the bolt all the way into the bottom end of the post. Then attach the gray plastic pieces to the two white plastic end caps, and insert the top end cap in the top of the post, placing the bottom piece on the floor approximately where you want to install the climbing pole.

Step 2: Marking the length of the post. Place the end of the bolt in the bottom piece, and move the post into position where you want it to be. Extend the post so the top end piece is snug against the ceiling, and use a pencil to mark the top of the outer post on the inner post.

Step 3: Preparing the post. Take down the post, and twist the two pieces until they no longer slide in and out, ensuring that the mark you just made stays at the top of the outer part. The next steps are little tricks that will help make the post sturdier when it's in place. Drill a pilot hole through both the outer and inner

climb this! creating the perfect floor-to-ceiling climbing pole

poles, and insert a small setscrew. This keeps the two parts from rotating. Repeat this same step at the top of the post, drilling through the post and the part of the plastic end cap that extends into the post. This prevents the whole pole from twisting around the end cap.

Step 4: Wrapping the rope. Starting at either end of the post, attach rope using hot glue. Continue gluing and wrapping the rope all the way around the post until it is covered. Pull the rope firmly as you glue it to be sure there are no gaps between each wrap. When you reach the end, cut the rope with scissors or a utility knife, and secure the end to the pole with a dab of hot glue.

KATE'S PRO TIPS

You don't have to glue every inch of the rope to the post, but I find that if you don't, the rope will stretch and sag over time, leaving unsightly gaps. I highly recommend gluing the whole thing!

Step 5: Final installation. Put the wrapped pole back in position, and use a level on all sides to be sure it's perfectly vertical. Once you have the pole positioned properly, follow the instructions that came with the Stolmen post, and adjust the bottom bolt to add extra tension between the floor and ceiling. This keeps the pole in place. It's a good idea to have one person hold the pole while another person adjusts the bolt. The final, and optional, step is to drill three screws through the holes in the top end piece and into the ceiling. This secures the pole and keeps it from possibly spinning.

KATE'S PRO TIPS

Sisal and manila rope fray easily at the ends. A trick I learned is to take a piece of twine and wrap it securely around the end of the rope at both ends. Tie a knot and tuck in the ends. This prevents the main rope from fraying and has a nice aesthetic that matches the look of the climbing pole.

cats on the ceiling

CAT GUARDIANS WITH ELEVEN CATS GET SOME SQUARE FOOTAGE BACK

SUBMITTED BY:
Enno Wolf and
Aïda Renout;
Almere, The Netherlands

CATS:
Mika, Salo, Snuit, Casper,
Joop, Olivier, Bob, Harry,
Pieter, Tommy, and Ricky

With eleven cats, our house was cluttered with scratching posts and cat trees. We asked ourselves, What if they could use the ceiling? How could we hang everything up there? So we decided to create a whole playground suspended from the ceiling where the cats could climb and hang out.

We used premade cat climbing furniture from Quality Cat (qualitycat -krabpalen.nl), but we did something with it the manufacturer had never seen or even thought of. We drilled 50 holes into the concrete ceiling from which to hang the sisal columns and suspend the platforms. We made sure we could hang from each column to ensure that they were strong enough to hold the weight of the cats.

The Result

It's like the cats have their own floor now, and we have our living room back. The only downside is that we have to use a ladder to clean the walkways.

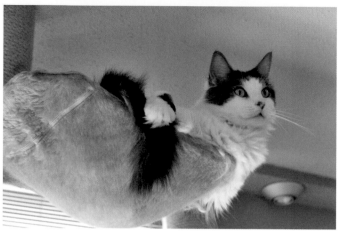

First of all, I applaud how Enno and Aïda took an off-the-shelf product and really made it their own—super creative! Of course, with any design like this, I have to ask: What happens if there's a catfight up there? How do you get them down when you have to? That's the only thing that worries me a little bit, but this is a nice example of out-of-the-box Catification. Don't tell me you don't have room for a superhighway; you have a ceiling!

I agree—what an ingenious use of an existing product! I bet the manufacturer was blown away. I also like how Enno and Aïda used the full cat trees to create on/off ramps for the ceiling walkway. The trees offer lots of resting spots at different levels, too. It must be so much fun to watch the cats while they are overhead.

creating a catio

Outdoor enclosures for cats—also known as catios—are a great way to let your cats enjoy the outdoors without exposing them to the potential dangers they would face if allowed to roam freely. Catios range from small enclosures to elaborate screened-in rooms. You can really let your imagination and creativity go wild when planning a catio (of course, within the limits set by your landlord or homeowner's association!). When making your Catification plan, consider how you might give your cat protected access to the outside by expanding your home to include a catio.

Catios, to me, are the great compromise. While Kate and I are (literally!) begging people to not let their cats outside, we still believe there are ways to allow cats to have access to fresh air and sunshine, to see birds and bugs, and to experience a little bit of what comes with outdoor living. An excellent way to make this happen is through the magic of a catio. Any structure, from elaborate full-size catios to small window enclosures, allows for this compromise to take place. However much space you can allocate, remember that you are expanding your cat's territory—which is a very good thing.

Catios are like Catification laboratories. Because it's not actually your living room or your bedroom, it becomes a place where you can experiment and test things to find out how far you're willing to go in your efforts to create an environment that is happy and healthy for both human and feline.

Behaviorally, catios help cats organically cross their own challenge line; like any Catification project, catios should be scalable and filled with everything from scent soakers (for comfort, both physical and territorial) to superhighway elements that can change over time to accommodate the cat's curiosity and maturation.

kate's catio

🐾 *Kate*

When I was shopping for a new home, I went with my Realtor to look at a nice little condo in central Phoenix, and the second I stepped out the sliding glass doors from the living room onto a partially open back patio with an old rotting roof structure overhead, I knew that was the one. I could see the potential for an incredible catio! The bones were already there; I just had to complete the picture and I would have the perfect indoor/outdoor space for my cats.

I tore down the old rotting beams and had

a friend help build an extension off the main roof and connect it to the tops of the existing block walls. We used metal mesh and a sturdy wood frame of 2×4s to make it completely secure. The mesh lets in plenty of light and air, but no critters can get in or out. The roof of the catio is industrial metal roofing material. I added some cat shelves and a covered area for the litter boxes, plus a sisal-wrapped climbing pole leading to the top shelves. As soon as it was finished, I let the cats out into their new catio and they loved it.

kate's catio

It Doesn't Have to Be Perfect!

 Kate

I installed the catio a few years ago, and now realize that I need to revisit it. As Jackson will be happy to point out, I have a dead end! The top shelf over the closet door leads nowhere. This just goes to show that even the experts can improve on their Catification plan! But it also serves to demonstrate that you have to try—come up with something and do it. Don't feel like it has to be perfect and complete right away. Your design can—actually, it should—evolve over time. Put up some shelves and watch what your cats do and then add on accordingly. I plan to extend our superhighway all the way around the catio to give the cats more places to run and climb.

Jackson

I think the thing that causes paralysis in Catification is the sense that you've got to get it all done at once, or it's a failure. Don't let your designer ego get in the way; remember, your cats will thank you for *anything* that gives them a greater sense of territory. Building the skeleton for your Catification is the main job, the rest is gravy.

Kate's Catio Tips

IT'S YOUR CATIO, TOO!

Be sure to include a mix of feline and human furniture so you can spend time on the catio with your cats when the weather is nice. Remember, it's for you, too!

ADD SOME EDIBLES

Cat grass and catnip plants are perfect additions to any catio. Be sure any plants you add to your catio are nontoxic and safe for cats. Visit aspca.org for a list of cat-safe plants.

MAKE IT SAFE

There are many different kinds of mesh or screen you can use to fence in a catio. Even basic chicken wire will do. Just be sure it can be securely fastened to the frame so there aren't any gaps where a cat might slip out.

Half-Round
Climbing Shelves

 Kate

I made these simple climbing shelves for my catio with 24-inch-diameter precut circular pieces of wood available at the home improvement store (look in the lumber section). I cut them in half, painted them with outdoor paint, and added decorative brackets to create perfect half-round perches.

SUBMITTED BY:
Carrie Fagerstrom;
Portland, Oregon

CATS:
Milo, Simon, Emma, Billy
Boy, Chloe, Casper,
Celeste, Tai, and Ember

carrie's catio

Many of my older cats had been either indoor/outdoor or former street cats (one was even feral) before I decided they should all live indoors only. I wanted them to be able to enjoy the outdoors safely, and I hoped that Simon and Milo could move back in from the front porch, where they had been relocated to after three months of spraying in protest of the new rules. It worked!

AFTER

Carrie's project is similar to mine in that she also found a home with terrific "catio potential." She just had to have vision to imagine the possibilities. I like how Carrie used the clear panels for the roof. It lets in lots of sunshine but still keeps out the rain—especially important in Portland! She and I both used the banana leaf footstools from IKEA. These are great for a catio because they're designed for outdoor use and the texture is really attractive to cats. I assumed my cats would scratch the footstools to bits, but they just love to sit on them.

No-Excuses Catification:
Easy Cat Fountain

Here's a really easy way to add a water feature to your catio. All you need is a basic aquarium pump with a filter (here we used a ten-gallon aquarium pump with a charcoal filter, available from a pet supply store for $10 to $15) and a bowl or other container. Simply assemble the pump according to the directions, insert the filter cartridge, hang the pump on the side of the bowl, fill the bowl with water, prime the pump by filling it with water too, plug it in, and let your cat enjoy her new water fountain!

Kate

You can do this with all different kinds of bowls or containers; just find one that allows the filter to hang on the edge so the water falls into the bowl. I used a vintage bowl I had sitting on my kitchen counter. It's better if the sides of the bowl are straight up and down, rather than at an angle, so the filter will sit upright, but if the sides of your bowl are angled, you can place a small shim between the outside of the bowl and the filter to make it fit better.

Use a ceramic, glass, or stainless-steel container

if possible. These materials can be thoroughly cleaned and won't scratch, while plastic can scratch over time and harbor bacteria that might cause feline acne. Be sure to clean your fountain regularly!

Did you know that it's better to place your cat's water bowl far away from their food bowl? In nature, cats instinctively do not drink water that is near a food source because there is a chance that the water could be contaminated. This is also why some cats prefer to drink moving water, like from a fountain or from the faucet. Moving water is less likely to be contaminated than stagnant water. Try adding a cat drinking fountain, or at least move your cat's water dish to another area that's away from her food bowl. You might find that she drinks more water!

autumn's atrium

A Behind-the-Scenes Look
at *My Cat from Hell*,
Season 4, Episode 6

You may remember Jackson's trip to San Francisco when he helped Deb and Brian and their two kids, Brendan and Erin, with their cat, Autumn. Part of the Catification plan for Autumn included creating an awesome catio for her in the existing atrium. The giant tree growing in the middle of the atrium provided the perfect centerpiece for Autumn's new indoor/outdoor playground.

Autumn was an inquisitive teenager who wanted to run and play, but she had recently gotten lost outside and the experience had traumatized her. That's why I was there. We needed to expand her territory and give her a safe place to hang out and burn off some of that kitten energy.

Upon walking through Deb and Brian's front door, I walked straight into the atrium and thought, Holy sweet catio! I didn't care what else we were doing in this house; I knew we were going to make them a catio for sure. The first thing you see is the tree that goes up right through the opening in the roof. The tree was a challenge—because we had to figure out how to prevent Autumn from climbing all the way out—but it was the best catio feature ever, because what better thing could you provide a young cat to climb and scratch on than a natural tree?

© 2014 Discovery Communications, LLC

Deb and Brian and the kids really took on the challenge of turning their atrium into a Catified space. They started by adding flashing to the top of each

tree limb. This prevents Autumn from climbing all the way up the tree and out onto the roof. She can't climb past the flashing because she can't get her claws into it. Brilliant!

They also added shelves, scratchers, beds, and cat grass plants to the tree, creating the most amazing kitty treehouse ever, really turning it into a destination for Autumn. They gave her scent soakers and things to keep her entertained, so now she has a place to explore and mark but she is safe and not able to escape.

PVC PIPE CAT FURNITURE

PVC pipes and fittings are like Tinkertoys for adults—you can build anything! And they're perfect for cat furniture, especially if it will be used outside on a catio, because PVC is sturdy and weather resistant. The materials are relatively inexpensive, construction is easy, and the possibilities are endless. Use your imagination, and put this versatile system to work for your next Catification project.

© Kate Benjamin

© Kate Benjamin

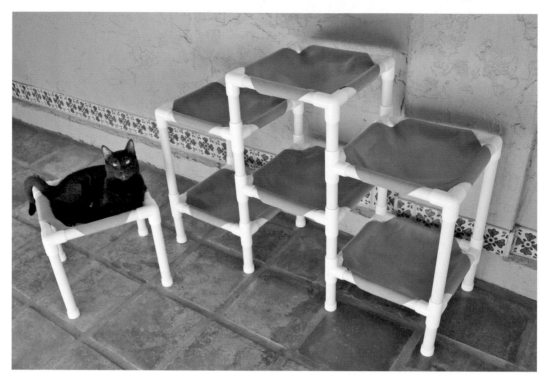

PVC PIPE

PVC pipe comes in different diameters, ranging from ½ inch to 2 inches or larger. You'll need to choose a size that is sturdy enough for your particular project. Usually ¾- or 1-inch-diameter pipe is suitable for cat furniture.

PVC FIXTURES

Several types of PVC fittings are available that allow you to attach the pipe in different configurations. Here are some of the most common fittings:

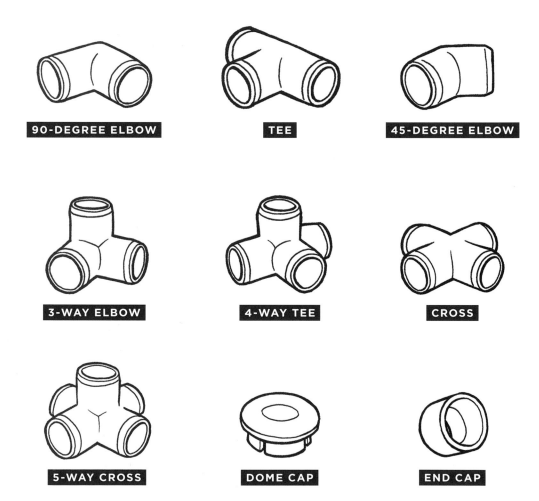

90-DEGREE ELBOW

TEE

45-DEGREE ELBOW

3-WAY ELBOW

4-WAY TEE

CROSS

5-WAY CROSS

DOME CAP

END CAP

FURNITURE-GRADE PVC

If you head to the home improvement store to purchase your PVC pipe and fittings, you'll notice that both usually have printing on the outside that won't come off. If you don't want the printing and other marks to show on your finished project, you can always paint the pipe and fittings, but you'll have to sand all the surfaces first and then use paint that is specially formulated for plastic. Or you can look for furniture-grade PVC pipe and fittings. These parts do not have any printing and sometimes come in colors other than black and white. Furniture-grade PVC parts are available from specialty retailers and online.

CUTTING PVC PIPE

There are three ways to cut PVC pipe to the length you need: 1) hacksaw, 2) pipe cutter, or 3) miter saw.

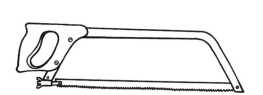

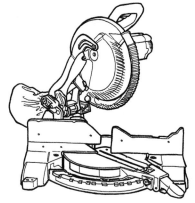

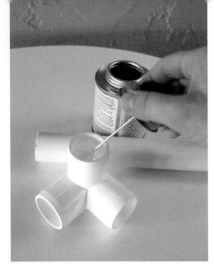

ATTACHING THE PIPE AND FITTINGS

When attaching the pipe to the fittings, you'll want to use PVC glue to secure the joints. Be sure to test-fit all your pieces before you glue them!

Every project will be different, and you may need to experiment with the types of connectors and the length of the pipe to get it right. Below are some examples of cat furniture projects made with 1-inch PVC pipe and fittings.

Easy Raised Cat Bed

Make a simple raised cat bed with one platform and four legs. Adjust the length of the legs to any height.

Parts:

8 (12-inch) pieces of 1-inch PVC pipe (make four shorter if you want to adjust the height)
4 end caps
4 three-way elbow connectors
1 fabric cover

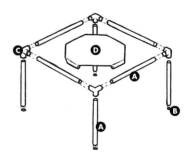

A 12" PVC PIPE

B END CAP

C 3-WAY ELBOW

D FABRIC COVER

Medium Cat Climber

It's easy to create levels with your PVC cat furniture project. Think about how cats can move from one level to the next when planning your design.

Parts:

20 (6-inch) pieces of 1-inch PVC pipe

24 (12-inch) pieces of 1-inch PVC pipe

4 (13½-inch) pieces of 1-inch PVC pipe

8 end caps

16 four-way Tee connectors

8 three-way elbow connectors

6 fabric covers

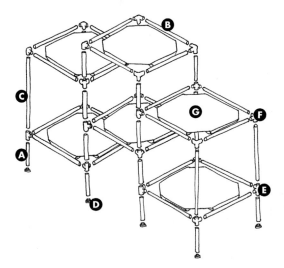

A 6" PVC PIPE

B 12" PVC PIPE

C 13.5" PVC PIPE

D END CAP

E 4-WAY TEE

F 3-WAY ELBOW

G FABRIC COVER

Deluxe Cat Activity Center

Let your imagination go wild and design a whole activity center for your cats with multiple levels, built-in scratchers, and hanging toys!

Parts:

36 (6-inch) pieces of 1-inch PVC pipe

42 (12-inch) pieces of 1-inch PVC pipe

4 (13½-inch) pieces of 1-inch PVC pipe

4 (24-inch) pieces of 1-inch PVC pipe

28 four-way Tee connectors

12 three-way elbow connectors

4 Tee connectors

12 end caps

9 fabric covers

1 fleece hammock

Sisal rope for scratching posts

2 hanging cat toys

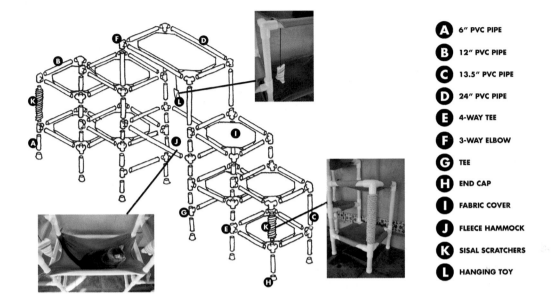

- **A** — 6" PVC PIPE
- **B** — 12" PVC PIPE
- **C** — 13.5" PVC PIPE
- **D** — 24" PVC PIPE
- **E** — 4-WAY TEE
- **F** — 3-WAY ELBOW
- **G** — TEE
- **H** — END CAP
- **I** — FABRIC COVER
- **J** — FLEECE HAMMOCK
- **K** — SISAL SCRATCHERS
- **L** — HANGING TOY

MAKING THE FABRIC COVERS

Here's a simple way to make the fabric covers for the platforms of your PVC cat furniture. You'll want to use a heavy canvas fabric. If your cat furniture will be outside on a catio, pick an outdoor fabric that's water and sun resistant. The dimensions will vary for each project, but here's an example to get you started.

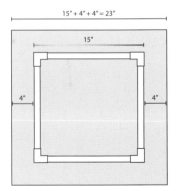

Step 1. Cut your fabric large enough to extend beyond your frame 4 inches on all four sides. For example, if your frame measures 15 inches by 15 inches, cut your fabric 23 inches by 23 inches (15 + 4 + 4 = 23).

pvc pipe cat furniture 251

Step 2. Fold the corners of the fabric over so the edge just shows at the corner of the frame. Iron to crease the fabric and trim the extra fabric, leaving 1 or 2 inches folded over.

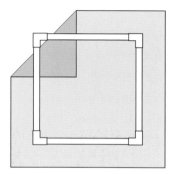 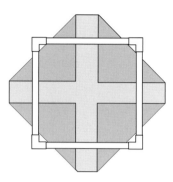 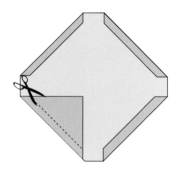

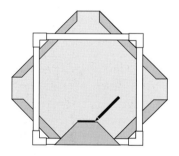

Step 3. Place the frame over the fabric, fold each side over the frame, and mark the edge of the fabric on the underside of the hammock.

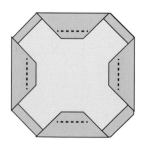

Step 4. Stitch along the edge of the folded fabric.

Step 5. Slide the PVC pipe through the pocket and attach with fittings at the corners.

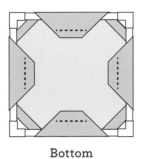

Bottom

Top

EASY NO-SEW HAMMOCK

If your sewing skills are lacking, there's another easy way to make a quick, no-sew hammock for your PVC cat furniture. Use a stretchy fabric that won't fray at the edges, like fleece. Cut the fabric long enough to extend beyond the edge of your frame by 4 inches on all four sides, cut a slit about 4 inches long in each corner, and simply tie the hammock in place. Note: This type of hammock only works on lower platforms where the pipe extends above on all four corners.

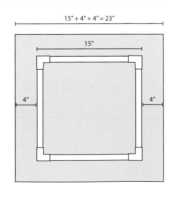

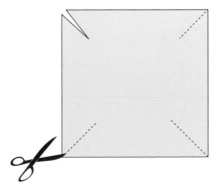

pvc pipe cat furniture **253**

ADDING A SISAL SCRATCHING POST

To give Kitty a place where she can leave her mark, think about adding a scratching surface to your project. Simply wrap any of the posts—either vertical or horizontal—with sisal rope. First drill a hole in the pipe that's slightly larger than the thickness of the rope you're using. (This example uses ⅜-inch rope and a ½-inch drill bit.) Feed the rope into the hole,

and wrap the rope around the pipe, using a hot-glue gun to secure the rope as you go. Drill another hole at the opposite end of the pipe, and tuck in the end of the rope. Be sure to leave enough pipe exposed to attach the connector.

ADDING A HANGING TOY

For extra fun, it's easy to add a hanging-toy or two to your project. Simply take one of Kitty's favorite toys, attach it to a length of shock cord or other string, and attach it to the PVC pipe. Place the toy slightly out of reach so Kitty will have to reach for it and bat it around. Pick a toy with catnip or a bell inside to make it extra interesting.

Here, we drilled a hole in the pipe and fed the end of the cord through the hole, tying a knot inside the pipe to keep the toy in place. You could also just tie the cord around the pipe.

pvc pipe cat furniture (255)

SUBMITTED BY:
Erin Clanton Cupp;
Cambria, Illinois

CATS:
Nubbins, Theodore,
Harriet, Sarah, Penny,
and Feller

the cupp house catwalk

Our Sarah has always been a "Nervous Nellie." I thought getting her more vertical would boost her confidence. Also, our Harriet gained quite a bit of weight after she was spayed, and we needed to get her more active. I wanted to build something that would be in keeping with our home's style and still be fun for our furry kids.

Materials and Budget

I used 1×10, 1×5, and 1×3 whitewood boards, paint, caulk, and lots and lots of screws. I purchased my supplies at a home improvement store. The whole project cost around $200.

Erin's Tips

It started with one board. I had a 1×10×8 board left over from another project and thought, why not? I didn't have any real plan at that point. I cut a triangle out of a piece of paper for a template and just started marking out pieces.

The staircase came about rather quickly and then I needed to design a destination for the staircase to lead to. This is where I started to plan, plan, plan. I wanted to be sure whatever I implemented blended well into our home's style. I researched many different architectural details and decided to fashion a wraparound ledge that mimicked the dentil moldings of Craftsman-style exterior design.

Regardless of your personal style or that of your home, there is no reason to believe that Catification must look a certain way. With a little brainstorming, you can transform a space into something that both you and your furry kids will love.

The Result

Our Harriet actually didn't wait until I was done with the superhighway to make her way all the way around. She had been "helping" me build it the whole time and tried out each section for me as I got it done to be sure I did it right.

Now that the whole build is complete, we have seen the cats take many laps around the room. There's nothing like the sound of a herd of clamoring elephants stampeding above your head! Mini-mice toys are perfect for throwing up there for the hunt, and our furry kids love to knock them down onto the top of our heads while we sit on the couch beneath them. They like to see how fast they can rocket up the stairs. We have also found that it is the perfect apparatus for "showing off for company." You know you are liked if you come by the Cupp house and one or three of them hop up there to strut their stuff.

Miss Sarah's confidence is up, and Miss Harriet, well, she embraces her size. Everyone's happy.

 *Jackson*

On the human side, I love the look of this and how beautifully it matches the house. I also love that it was clearly inspired by a deep love for the cats who live in this home.

It's a great example of Catification to show people who are "crazy cat lady"–phobic, to say, Hey, this is what you can do!

In terms of functionality for the cats, it looks to me like a potentially dangerous setup. I'd like to see carpeting on the shelves where the cats tend to sleep to prevent slipping. I'd also love to see an alternate ramp-style exit to give the cats a choice for how to reach the superhighway. If I were a Maine Coon and I had a choice between a spiral staircase and a ramp, I'd probably take the ramp. It's good to give the cats that choice.

 Kate

This is such a beautiful element, you really wouldn't guess it's for the cats at all. I'd say it's a great example of seamless Catification, because imagine reselling this house. Someone without cats would see this as a decorative feature for displaying plants or other objects. That's kind of a good test, if you're worried about over-Catifying. Ask yourself, could the elements be used by a homeowner without cats? If the answer is yes, then you've completely integrated your design. (Although I think every home should have a cat or two!)

thumbelina's turf war (and peace)

A Behind-the-Scenes Look at *My Cat from Hell*, Season 5, Episode 13

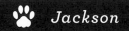 Jackson

Leilani and Michael had two tiny and docile Balinese cats, Thumbelina and Tinkerbell, who got along beautifully. Then came the day when they decided to add two F2 Savannahs named Tigger and Sahara to their family (!), at which point all hell promptly broke loose. There were constant conflicts among the cats. Ironically, these conflicts were usually started by Thumbelina, the smallest of the bunch. Talk about a Napoleon Cat! It doesn't get much more Napoleon than having a five-pound cat get territorially panicked and quell her anxiety by picking on a thirty-pound cat. Along with the fighting came a monumental amount of pee-

ing happening all over the house. As a matter of fact, for the first homework assignment, I had them place scent soakers everywhere to help the Balinese cats establish territorial ownership, and by the time I got back for the second visit, every single one had been soaked, but not in a good way. They were soaked with pee. Everything was backfiring. You have to remember, when you're dealing with a twenty-five- to thirty-pound hybrid cat, you're dealing with physical and mental needs beyond your wildest nightmares.

Although Leilani and Michael's two-story townhouse included a catio, the overall space was obviously not enough for these four cats. I suggested that they

Catify the living room. I gave them basic guidelines on what to do and returned later. They had built a mini-racetrack around the sliding glass door and added a cat tree next to it. While I was happy that they had tried at all, the truth is that they hadn't tried very hard. Considering that Michael is a carpenter and had all the skills to build something really nice, I was pretty disappointed in Leilani. She had pushed back pretty hard on the assignment, saying she had a very specific aesthetic and was afraid that the "crazy cat lady" design would ruin it. I was testing her commitment to her cats, and, to be honest, I felt that she had failed.

Then they told me that they had a surprise for me. They took me upstairs and POW! They had built a beautiful habitat for their cats in the office—an extremely socially significant room for their cats. Based on what I told them that their cats needed in this room, they came up with this design all on their own. I was so stunned that I nearly fell over! I walked into that room, and I was overcome by a true embodiment of Catification Nation—it was Catification in full effect. I had given them the tools and they had run with it. It's pretty stunning.

Everything about this design works. I asked for lanes of traffic, and I got a traffic circle in the ceiling. Michael even went into the attic to install support beams to attach the walkway. He actually demonstrated how strong it is by hanging from it himself. There are also on/off ramps all over the room, ways to allow the cats to come down to the floor and back up again. Every element of this project was

knocked out of the park. I was really proud of them for playing a major role in restoring sanity to their home. Michael and Leilani were then able to learn from what they had done in this Catification basecamp and expand that out through the rest of the house.

CAT DADDY DICTIONARY

BASECAMP

Basecamp is a room that becomes a territorial ground zero of sorts. In this room, scent soakers are placed strategically throughout. This goes for human as well as feline scents. A couch for you; a bed for them. A chair for you; a fleece-covered window perch for them. The mingling of scents gives them a deep sense of home. Bowls, litter boxes, and scratching posts all add up to create a world of Raw Cat serenity.

Basecamp is essential when moving to a new home of course, but it takes on a new dimension when applied to Catification. If an object has been solidified as socially significant within the confines of basecamp, it stands to reason that the object will hold equal importance when placed somewhere else in the home. Then you can add a new object inside the room to replace the old, and voilà! Through this "basecamp trade-out," you've created a territorial security factory!

SUBMITTED BY:
Karen Rae; San Diego,
California

CAT:
Zachary

the purrfect
cat bridge

Sometimes when your superhighway hits a dead end, you have to think like an urban planner. Take this example. There was a big gap between these two cabinets—a bit too far to jump—so Karen built a cat bridge to help Zachary get across the gap. The result is a beautiful architectural element that integrates seamlessly into the superhighway.

Catification Essentials

Some cats like to chew power cords, which could lead to an unthinkable outcome. Install cord protectors to prevent this behavior, and be sure to provide Kitty with plenty of toys and other stimulation as a substitute.

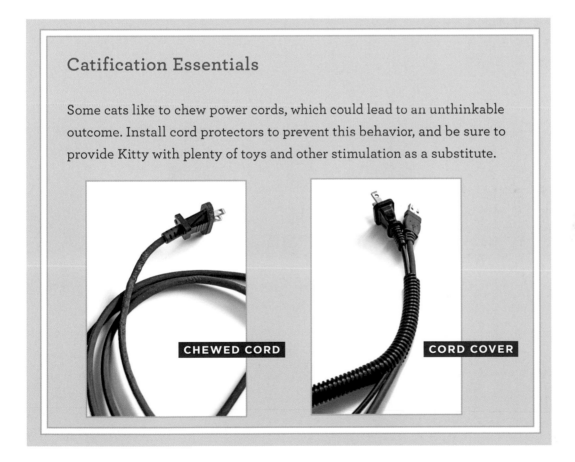

CHEWED CORD

CORD COVER

SUBMITTED BY:
Bob and Linda Stafford;
Wilderville, Oregon

CATS:
Sam and Norton

rustic bliss, feline style

BRINGING THE OUTDOORS INSIDE FOR YOUR CATS

We wanted to give the cats a tall structure to climb and lounge on and a high vantage point to observe the activities of the birds at the feeders just outside the window.

Materials and Budget

We live in the woods, and we've incorporated peeled logs in several projects around our home, including the staircase, so using the same material for this project was an obvious choice. We used plywood left over from another project for the shelves, topped them with surplus carpet that matches the floor, and added narrow wood trim around the edges to disguise the plywood. All we had to purchase were the shelf brackets and a bolt to attach the top of the post to a beam. Finally, we finished the bare wood with a coat of polyurethane. Total cost: less than $20.

Bob and Linda's Tips

We usually have a variety of peeled logs on hand, so all we had to do was select one that could be cut to the proper height for our space. This one also has an interesting growth (called a burl) on the top so we kept that and then we sanded the whole thing. We then cut out shelves with half-circles at the end of each to fit the log. After we attached carpet to each shelf and mounted the shelves with brass brackets, we added some small peeled branches for extra support. Finally, we attached some carpeted planks to the bottom for scratching that can be easily removed and re-carpeted when they become thoroughly shredded.

The Result

The cats didn't immediately climb on it; they may have thought it was just another piece of furniture they weren't supposed to jump up on. So we enticed them up with a variety of toys and then they seemed to realize that this tree was just for them. They love the view from up there, and they can see what's going on upstairs and down. The

top shelf is a little larger than the others so that's a favorite place to lie down and take a nap. We're very happy with how it turned out. It blends in nicely with the stairs, and the boys have their own indoor tree to climb and hang out on.

🐾 Jackson

This piece works for both the human aesthetic and feline functionality. Take a look at how seamlessly it fits into the décor of their home, yet it serves a purpose by creating a killer vantage point of the downstairs, as well as the comings and goings from upstairs to down. Best of all, because it uses nature in the same way it's used in the surrounding architecture, it's a piece they don't have to aesthetically apologize for, hence the front and center position in the home.

Now let's take it a step further. Bob and Linda have created a great vantage point for their cats to enjoy, but it doesn't lead anywhere. What if the top shelf of the tree led around the room at the level of the beam? Then maybe another shelf going up the stairs? I mean, why not? Especially if you add another cat or two to your home. (Hint, hint!)

I agree; they did a great job matching the cat tree to the aesthetic of their home. I also like the thought that went into the carpeted scratch pads; making them easily removable so they can be recovered as needed is an excellent idea. Anything that cats are going to scratch will need to be replaced over time, so it's important to work that in to your Catification plan from the beginning.

conclusion

We've given you much homework throughout *Catification*, but we had our own, very demanding homework as well when we undertook this project. We wanted to wow and inspire you, whether you are a fanatical "cat person" or someone who "has a cat," whether you live in a mansion or a studio, in an urban, suburban, or rural environment . . . like we said, *very* demanding homework for us!

And now, the final exam for all of us:

Your cat walks into the room, looks toward the mantle, and meows. Do you:

a. Worry about the priceless vase she's about to knock over?

b. Ignore her and think about dinner?

c. Think about how to connect the mantle to the bookcase to the cat tree by the window for your tree dweller?

Out of four cats in your home, one has taken to spending most of the day under the bed. Do you:

a. Assume she knows what she wants out of life and leave her alone?
b. Try to make life a bit more comfy for her by putting extra bedding down there and making sure it's vacuumed?
c. Push her challenge line, block off "the unders," and give her cocoons of all shapes and sizes to show her a brave new world?

One of your cats has taken to repeatedly peeing in the corner of your dining room. Do you:

a. Clean it up every time, muttering under your breath about how much you do for them and how much they hate you in return?
b. Use the tried-and-true method of moving a chair on top of it, plugging in an air freshener nearby, and pretending it never happened?
c. Think of a way to add a litter box in the corner that you can live with aesthetically and that the cat will actually use?

You pass! As a graduation present, we'd like to present you with a shiny new pair of cat glasses! Use these glasses to solve problems and prevent them from happening in the first place. Every time your cat walks into the room from today on, you should feel secure in your knowledge of what she wants, what she's up to, and, just as if she were your human child, how you can balance comfort and challenge to allow her to be the greatest version of herself that she can be.

Cat glasses assist you but what we know you have—the heart of a guardian—guides you. The inspiration and the perspiration, the fascination and endless curiosity, and of course, the unconditional love you feel for one another—these intangibles complete the Catification toolbox.

We hope that as you get more fluent in the language of Catification, you also remember to pay it forward; every idea that you have, if shared, could help another cat guardian you might never meet, somewhere in the world, with their own "situation." You can prevent the kind of frustration that leads humans to the end of their rope, and leads cats to the shelter. Through shared ideas, ingenuity, and passion, together we can save and enrich lives. At the beginning of this journey, we invited you to first know all cats, then, know yours. Now, by sharing your knowledge and commitment to making your cat happy in your home, you can help make all of them happy and ensure they all have homes.

acknowledgments

Kate and Jackson would like to thank the following people and organizations for their shared commitment and dedication to a strange, wonderful, and important idea. From the inspiration to the perspiration, for this dedication and beyond, we truly honor and appreciate them for allowing us to guide them blindfolded through the Catified wilderness.

Sara Carder and her team at Tarcher/Penguin, including Joanna Ng, Brianna Yamashita, Claire Vaccaro, and Meighan Cavanaugh.

Joy Tutela and Luke Thomas at David Black Agency.

Rebecca Brooks and team at Brooks Group PR, including Niki Turkington, Lindsay Smith, and Esther McIlvain.

Josephine Tan, Kevin Krogstad, and Jessica Hano at Tan Management.

To Animal Planet, Discovery Communications, and Eyeworks USA, without whom the word Catification would never have been spoken in millions of homes around the world.

To all of the 100-plus cats and their families who have thus far opened their homes and hearts on *My Cat from Hell*.

To the very heart of #TeamCatMojo, Siena Lee-Tajiri, Toast Tajiri, and Heather Curtis.

To Norm Aladjem, Carolyn Conrad, and Ivo Fischer and their teams at LEG, Schreck,

Rose, Dapello & Adams, and William Morris/Endeavor for helping to steer The Good Ship Mojo.

To those who worked on the day-to-day reality that was the making of this book: Catherine Madrid and Nica Scott for the beautiful illustrations you see throughout the book; Linda Pelo for her administrative assistance and for keeping us organized throughout this process; Susan Weingartner, Joanne McGonagle, Peter Wolf, and Ingrid King for their help along the way.

To everyone in Catification Nation for their submissions, ideas, and inspiration for this book.

To the cats who made up our feline focus group and reminded us why we do this every day. Let's go alphabetically—in Jackson's house: Barry, Caroline, Chuppy, Eddie, Lily, Oliver, Pishi, Sophie, and Velouria; and in Kate's house and studio: Ando, Andy, Bear, Claude, Dazzler, Flora, Lilly, Mackenzie, Mama Cat, Margot, McKinley, Ratso Katso, Sherman, Simba, and Sylvia.

SPECIAL THANKS

From Jackson:

To Minoo, true north and twin flame.

From Kate:

To my team at the Hauspanther studio, Gerda Lobo, Star DeLuna, and Sara Santiago; to my parents, Don and Barbara Benjamin, for following along this crazy adventure from the beginning; and to Mark, for helping take care of the crew while I was working on this project and for loving them as much as I do.

index

photo and illustration credits

Page ii: Photo by Rebecca Brittain

Page iii: Photo by Kate Benjamin

Pages 18–20: Illustrations by Nica Scott

Page 46: Illustration by Nica Scott

Page 55 collage:

CAT: MAKI	CAT: ZACHARY	CAT: TED
Guardian: Edith Esquivel Eguiguren	*Guardian:* Karen Rae	*Guardians:* Ryan and Lizzie Lewis
Location: Cuernavaca, Morelos, Mexico	*Location:* San Diego, California	*Location:* Santa Monica, California
	Photographer: Colleen's Custom Pet Photography	
CAT: PASHA	CAT: TOMMY	CAT: SUGAR
Guardian: Michelle Fehler	*Guardian:* Donna J. Crabtree	*Guardian:* All About Animals Rescue
Location: Phoenix, Arizona	*Location:* Tijeras, New Mexico	*Location:* Glendale, Arizona
	Photographer: David Murphy	*Photographer:* Kate Benjamin
CATS: L.T., LEON, AND SHERLOCK	CAT: TANOSHII	CAT: JEZEBEL
Guardians: John and Debi Congram	*Guardian:* Heidi Abrahamson	*Guardians:* Cheri and Naren Shankar
Location: Arlington Heights, Illinois	*Location:* Phoenix, Arizona	*Location:* Beverly Hills, California
		Photographer: Susan Weingartner Photography

Pages 68–69: Rendering and photos by Kate Benjamin

Page 70: Photo by Kate Benjamin. Illustration by Catherine Madrid.

Page 71: Photos by Kate Benjamin

Page 72: Illustration by Catherine Madrid

Pages 73–76: Photos by Kate Benjamin

Pages 78–82: Photos by Rebecca Brittain

Pages 86: Photo by Kate Benjamin

Pages 88–91: Photos by Kate Benjamin

Pages 92–93: (Top) Photo by Jackson Galaxy. All other photos by Kate Benjamin.

Pages 94–99: Photos by Sara

Pages 102–103: Illustrations by Catherine Madrid

Page 112: Photos by Kate Benjamin

Page 114: Photos by Kate Benjamin

Pages 117–119: Photos and illustrations by Rin Krak

Page 120: Photos by Peter Wolf and Kate Benjamin

Page 121 collage:

CAT: WOBBLY	CATS: SPORTY AND WALLABY	CAT: KEEPER
Guardians: Sara and Erik	*Guardian:* Kacy Turner	*Guardian:* Rebecca Mountain
Location: Minneapolis, Minnesota	*Location:* Fairfax, Virginia	*Location:* Orange, Massachusetts
CAT: EARL	CAT: PRECIOUS	CATS: PISHI AND GUS
Guardians: Matt and Diana Samberg	*Guardian:* Mandy Brannan	*Guardians:* Keith and Eileen Phillips
Location: Pittsburgh, Pennsylvania	*Location:* Cheyenne, Wyoming	*Location:* Madison, Alabama
CAT: BONEY MARONI	CAT: GRACIE	CAT: LUNA
Guardians: Dawn Kavanaugh and Mike Francis	*Guardians:* Dave and Kathleen Pickering	*Guardian:* Kim Pelaez
Location: Glendale, Arizona	*Location:* Danville, California	*Location:* Largo, Florida
Photographer: Kate Benjamin		

Pages 123–124: Photos by Nico & Katu

Page 125: Illustration by Catherine Madrid

Page 126: Photo by Nico & Katu

Pages 128–130: Photos by Kate Benjamin

Page 131: Photos by Kate Benjamin. Illustration by Catherine Madrid.

Pages 133–134: Photos by Wendy and David Hill

Page 134: Illustration by Catherine Madrid

Page 135 collage:

CAT: AMBER	CAT: SIDNEY	CAT: DORA
Guardian: Alinta Hawkins	*Guardian:* Mary Jane Chappell-Reed	*Guardians:* Linda and Tom Pelo
Location: Sarasota, Florida	*Location:* Lexington, Kentucky	*Location:* Parker, Colorado
CAT: PASHA	**CAT: MOMMY CAT**	**CAT: TONKS**
Guardian: Michelle Fehler	*Guardians:* Cheri and Naren Shankar	*Guardians:* Chuck and Cindy Schroyer
Location: Phoenix, Arizona	*Location:* Beverly Hills, California	*Location:* Morgan Hill, California
	Photographer: Susan Weingartner Photography	
CAT: TANOSHI	**CAT: FRIDA**	**CAT: ZEVY**
Guardian: Heidi Abrahamson	*Guardians:* Leyla Menchola and Julissa Menchola	*Guardians:* Dawn Kavanaugh and Mike Francis
Location: Phoenix, Arizona	*Location:* Callao, Peru	*Location:* Glendale, Arizona

Pages 136–139: Photos by Jenne Johnson

Page 139: Illustration by Catherine Madrid

Page 140: Photos by Kate Benjamin

Page 141: Photo by Peter Wolf

Pages 142–146: Photos by Marjorie Darrow and Ryan Davis

Page 150: Photo by Kate Benjamin

Pages 152–153: Rendering and photos by Kate Benjamin

Pages 156–157: Photos by Kate Benjamin

Page 158: Photos by Kate Benjamin. Illustration by Catherine Madrid.

Page 159: Photos by Kate Benjamin

Pages 160–161: Photos by Sylvia Jonathan

Page 162: Illustrations by Catherine Madrid

Pages 163–166: Photos and illustrations by Kate Benjamin

Page 167 collage:

CATS: MINGAU AND OLIVIA	CATS: CAPTAIN ROUGHY AND GILLIGAN	CAT: MAUR
Guardians: Cynthia Thompson and Diogenes Savi Mondo	*Guardian:* Lynn Maria Thompson	*Guardian:* Wendy Kaplan
Location: Porto Alegre, Brazil	*Location:* Neptune Beach, Florida	*Location:* Fort Lauderdale, Florida
CAT: MANGROVE	CAT: GOOGLE	CAT: ABBY
Guardians: Jane and Bud	*Guardians:* Candace Porth and Tony DiGiovine	*Guardians:* Toni and Mark Nicholson
Location: Portsmouth, Virginia	*Location:* Phoenix, Arizona	*Location:* Hartselle, Alabama
CAT: BUFFY	CAT: PASHA	CAT: AMELIA
Guardian: Melissa Claire Burgan	*Guardian:* Michelle Fehler	*Guardian:* Peter Wolf
Location: Milwaukee, Wisconsin	*Location:* Phoenix, Arizona	*Location:* Phoenix, Arizona

Pages 169–170: Photos by Lucio Castro

Pages 174–175: Photos by Kate Benjamin

Pages 176–177: Rendering and photos by Kate Benjamin

Pages 178–189: Photos and illustrations by Kate Benjamin

Pages 190–193: Photos by Michelle Tan Julius

Page 192: Illustrations by Catherine Madrid

Pages 194–195: Photos by Kate Benjamin

Pages 196–198: Photos by Marccello Pistilli

Pages 208–220: Rendering and photos by Kate Benjamin

Page 221 collage:

CAT: SQUATTER	CAT: DORA	CAT: KUNG FU TIGER LILY
Guardians: Denna Beena and Travis Fillmen	*Guardians:* Linda and Tom Pelo	*Guardians:* Mary and David Murphy
Location: Orlando, Florida	*Location:* Parker, Colorado	*Location:* Austin, Texas
CAT: OLIVER	CAT: MAUR	CAT: HEISENBERG
Guardians: Dana and Roger Rzepka	*Guardian:* Wendy Kaplan	*Guardian:* Mike Wilson
Location: Homer Glen, Illinois	*Location:* Fort Lauderdale, Florida	*Location:* Grand Rapids, Michigan
CAT: NALA	CAT: MARMIE	CAT: CRACKER
Guardian: Keely F.	*Guardians:* Vanessa Curry and Kevin Ressler	*Guardians:* Patrick and Johnida Dockens
Location: Fairfax, Virginia	*Location:* Mesa, Arizona	*Location:* Mesa, Arizona

Pages 222–225: Photos by Enno Wolf

Pages 226–233: Photos by Kate Benjamin

Pages 234–236: Photos by Carrie Fagerstrom

Pages 237–238: Photos by Kate Benjamin

Pages 244: Photo by Kate Benjamin

Page 245: Photo by Kate Benjamin. Illustration by Catherine Madrid.

Page 246: Illustrations by Catherine Madrid

Pages 247–250: Photos by Kate Benjamin. Illustrations by Catherine Madrid.

Pages 251–252: Photos and illustrations by Kate Benjamin

Page 253: Photo and illustrations by Kate Benjamin.

Pages 254–255: Photos by Kate Benjamin

Pages 256–259: Photos by Erin Clanton Cupp

Page 267: Photos by Kate Benjamin

Pages 269–270: Photos by Bob and Linda Stafford